Chapter 1: Introduction to VBA

Welcome to **"Solving problems in Microsoft Office 2024 and 365 using VBA and macros"**. This book is your comprehensive guide to enhancing and automating your Microsoft Office experience using Visual Basic for Applications (VBA) and macros. Whether you're a beginner or an experienced user, you'll find practical solutions to common problems and discover ways to optimize your workflow across Excel, Word, PowerPoint, and Outlook.

Why VBA and macros?

VBA and macros are powerful tools that allow you to automate repetitive tasks, create custom functions, and develop complex applications within the Microsoft Office suite. By mastering these tools, you can save time, reduce errors, and increase your productivity. This book will provide you with the knowledge and skills to tackle various challenges and improve your efficiency with practical examples and case studies.

What You will learn?

In this book, you will learn how to:

- Automate routine tasks in Excel, Word, PowerPoint, and Outlook.

- Create custom ribbons, toolbars, and user forms to enhance the user interface.

- Integrate data between different Office applications seamlessly.

- Develop robust error handling and debugging techniques.

- Optimize your VBA code for better performance.

- Solve real-world problems with practical case studies.

Who this book is for?

This book is designed for anyone who uses Microsoft Office 2024 and 365 and wants to harness the power of VBA and macros to solve problems and automate tasks. Whether you're an accountant, data analyst, project manager, or just someone looking to streamline their daily tasks, this book is for you.

How to use this book?

Each chapter is structured to build your knowledge progressively. Start with the basics of VBA and gradually move on to more advanced topics. The case studies and real-world examples at the end of the book provide practical applications of the concepts covered.

Feel free to skip to the sections that are most relevant to your needs. Use the examples as a reference and adapt the code to fit your specific scenarios.

1. Getting started with VBA in Excel

Welcome to the exciting world of VBA (Visual Basic for Applications)! If you're looking to supercharge your Excel skills, you've come to the right place. VBA lets you automate repetitive tasks, create powerful macros, and enhance Excel's functionality to fit your needs perfectly. Let's dive in and get started.

Writing your first macro

Step 1: Open Excel and access the Developer Tab

First things first, make sure you can see the Developer tab in Excel (below).

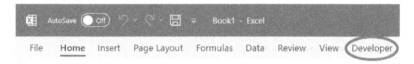

If it's not visible, you'll need to enable it:

1. Go to *File -> Options*.

2. In the *Excel Options* window, select *Customize Ribbon*.

3. Check the box next to *Developer* in the right pane and click *OK*.

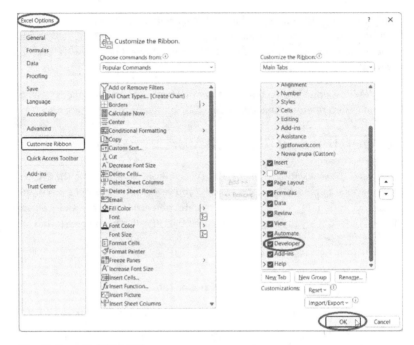

Step 2: Open the VBA Editor

With the Developer tab now visible, let's open the VBA editor:

1. Click on the *Developer* tab.

2. Click on *Visual Basic* in the *Code* group. This opens the VBA editor, where all the magic happens.

Step 3: Create a New Macro

1. In the VBA editor, go to *Insert -> Module*. This creates a new module where you can write your macro.

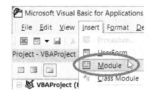

2. In the module window, type the following code:

```
Sub HelloWorld()
MsgBox "Hello, World!"
End Sub
```

This simple macro, named HelloWorld, will display a message box with the text "Hello, World!".

Step 4: Run Your Macro

1. Close the VBA editor and return to Excel.

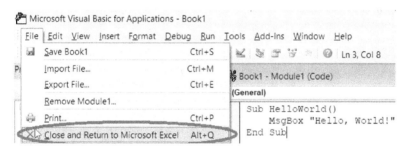

2. In the *Developer* tab, click *Macros*.

3. In the *Macro* dialog box, select *HelloWorld* and click *Run*.

You should see a message box that says "Hello, World!" Congrats, you've just written and executed your first VBA macro!

Using the VBA editor

The VBA editor is your playground for writing, testing, and debugging your macros. Here are some key features to help you get comfortable:

- **Project Explorer**: This is like the file explorer for your VBA projects. It shows all open workbooks and their associated modules, forms, and sheets.

- **Code Window**: This is where you write your VBA code. Each module or sheet has its own code window.

- **Immediate Window**: This handy tool lets you test code snippets on the fly and see results immediately.

Exploring the VBA Editor

1. **Project Explorer**: On the left side, you'll see the Project Explorer. It lists all the open workbooks and their contents. You can double-click on any item (like Sheet1 or Module1) to view its code.

2. **Properties Window**: Below the Project Explorer, you'll find the Properties window. This shows properties for the selected item, which can be useful for forms and controls.

3. **Code Window**: The main area where you write and edit your code. You can have multiple code windows open at once, each corresponding to different modules or sheets.

4. **Immediate Window**: You can activate this by pressing *Ctrl + G* or going to *View -> Immediate Window*. This is great for testing small code snippets and debugging.

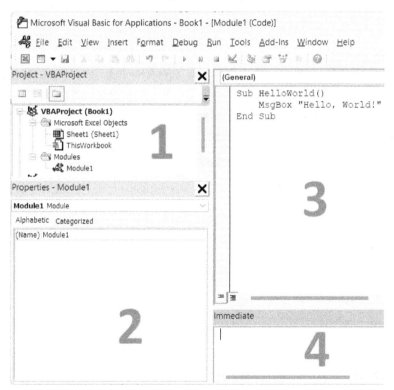

Basic navigation tips

- **Indent your code**: Use the *Tab* key to indent your code. This makes it easier to read, especially when dealing with loops and conditional statements.

- **Comment Your Code**: Use an apostrophe (') to add comments. Comments are ignored by VBA but are incredibly helpful for explaining what your code does.

```
Sub HelloWorld()
    ' This macro displays a message box with the text "Hello,
World!"
    MsgBox "Hello, World!"
End Sub
```

```
(General)

Sub HelloWorld()
    ' This macro displays a message box with the text "Hello, World!"
    MsgBox "Hello, World!"
End Sub
```

- **Run Your Code**: You can run your code from the VBA editor by pressing F5 or by clicking the Run button (the green play button).

By now, you should have a basic understanding of how to get started with VBA in Excel. You've written your first macro and explored the VBA editor. With these fundamentals, you're ready to delve deeper into the world of VBA and start automating your tasks like a pro!

2. Understanding the basics

Now that you've dipped your toes into VBA with your first macro, it's time to dive a bit deeper. In this section, we'll cover some fundamental concepts: variables and data types, and control structures like If, For, and While. These are the building blocks you'll use to create powerful and flexible macros.

Variables and data types

What is a variable? Think of a variable as a storage box where you can keep data that your macro needs. You can store numbers, text, dates, and more. To use a variable, you first need to declare it.

Declaring variables

To declare a variable, you use the *Dim* statement followed by the variable name and the data type. Here's a simple example:

```
Dim message As String
message = "Hello, VBA!"
MsgBox message
```

In this example:

- *Dim* stands for "Dimension" and is used to declare a variable.

- message is the name of the variable.

- As String tells VBA that this variable will store text (a string).

Common Data Types

- *String*: Stores text. Example: "*Hello, VBA!*"

- *Integer*: Stores whole numbers. Example: *42*

- *Double*: Stores decimal numbers. Example: *3.14*

- *Boolean*: Stores *True* or *False*.

Here's how you might use different data types:

```
Dim name As String
Dim age As Integer
Dim height As Double
```

```
Dim isStudent As Boolean

name = "Alice"
age = 25
height = 5.7
isStudent = True
```

Control structures (If, For, While)

Control structures are like the traffic signals for your code. They help you control the flow of your macro based on certain conditions or repeat actions multiple times.

If statements

The If statement lets you execute code only if a certain condition is true.

```
Dim score As Integer
score = 85

If score >= 90 Then
    MsgBox "A grade"
ElseIf score >= 80 Then
    MsgBox "B grade"
Else
    MsgBox "C grade or lower"
End If
```

In this example:

- If *score* is 90 or higher, it displays "A grade".

- If *score* is between 80 and 89, it displays "B grade".

- Otherwise, it displays "C grade or lower".

For loops

A *For* loop lets you repeat a block of code a specific number of times.

```
Dim i As Integer

For i = 1 To 5
```

```
            MsgBox "This is loop number " & i
    Next i
```

While loops

A *While* loop keeps running as long as a certain condition is true.

```
    Dim counter As Integer
    counter = 1

    While counter <= 5
        MsgBox "Counter is at " & counter
        counter = counter + 1
    end
```

In this example, the message box will appear five times, just like with the *For* loop. The loop stops when *counter* exceeds 5.

Putting it all together

Let's combine what we've learned into a more complex example. Suppose you want to create a macro that checks a list of students' scores and categorizes them.

```
    Sub CategorizeScores()
        Dim i As Integer
        Dim score As Integer
        Dim result As String

        For i = 1 To 10 ' Assume we have 10 scores
            score = Cells(i, 1).Value ' Get score from column
    A

            If score >= 90 Then
                result = "A"
            ElseIf score >= 80 Then
                result = "B"
            ElseIf score >= 70 Then
                result = "C"
            ElseIf score >= 60 Then
                result = "D"
```

```
        Else
            result = "F"
        End If


        Cells(i, 2).Value = result ' Output result in
column B
        Next i
    End Sub
```

In this macro:

- We loop through the first 10 rows in column A to get students' scores.

- We use an *If* statement to categorize each score.

- We store the result in column B next to each score.

Below code

```
(General)
    Sub CategorizeScores()
        Dim i As Integer
        Dim score As Integer
        Dim result As String

        For i = 1 To 10 ' Assume we have 10 scores
            score = Cells(i, 1).Value ' Get score from column A

            If score >= 90 Then
                result = "A"
            ElseIf score >= 80 Then
                result = "B"
            ElseIf score >= 70 Then
                result = "C"
            ElseIf score >= 60 Then
                result = "D"
            Else
                result = "F"
            End If

            Cells(i, 2).Value = result ' Output result in column B
        Next i
    End Sub
```

and result

A1						fx	
	A		B		C		D
1		F					
2		F					
3		F					
4		F					
5		F					
6		F					
7		F					
8		F					
9		F					
10		F					
11							

By understanding variables, data types, and control structures, you've got the foundational skills needed to start creating more complex and useful macros. Keep practicing, and soon you'll be automating your Excel tasks like a pro!

Chapter 2: Automating Excel tasks

3. Data manipulation

When it comes to working with Excel, one of the most powerful uses of VBA is to manipulate data. This includes importing data from various sources and exporting data for use elsewhere. Let's explore how to handle these tasks with VBA.

Importing and exporting data

Importing data from a text file

Sometimes you have data in a text file that you need to bring into Excel. Here's how you can do it:

```vba
Sub ImportTextFile()
    Dim filePath As String
    Dim textLine As String
    Dim rowNumber As Integer

    filePath = "C:\path\to\your\file.txt" ' Specify your
file path here
    rowNumber = 1 ' Start importing at the first row

    Open filePath For Input As #1 ' Open the text file for
reading

    Do Until EOF(1) ' Loop until the end of the file
        Line Input #1, textLine ' Read a line of text
        Cells(rowNumber, 1).Value = textLine ' Write the
line to the first column
        rowNumber = rowNumber + 1 ' Move to the next row
    Loop

    Close #1 ' Close the text file
End Sub
```

In this example:

- We open a text file and read it line by line.
- Each line is written to a new row in the first column of the Excel sheet.
- This simple loop continues until all lines in the file are read.

Importing data from another workbook

Sometimes, you need to pull data from another Excel workbook. Here's how:

```
Sub ImportFromWorkbook()
    Dim sourceWorkbook As Workbook
    Dim sourceSheet As Worksheet
    Dim targetSheet As Worksheet

    ' Define the source and target workbooks and sheets
    Set targetSheet = ThisWorkbook.Sheets("Sheet1")
    Set sourceWorkbook =
Workbooks.Open("C:\path\to\your\sourceWorkbook.xlsx")
    Set sourceSheet = sourceWorkbook.Sheets("Sheet1")

    ' Copy data from source to target
    sourceSheet.Range("A1:C10").Copy
Destination:=targetSheet.Range("A1")

    ' Close the source workbook
    sourceWorkbook.Close SaveChanges:=False
End Sub
```

In this example:

- We open another workbook and specify the worksheet we want to copy from.
- We copy a range of data from the source worksheet to the target worksheet.
- After copying, we close the source workbook.

Exporting data to a text file

Exporting data from Excel to a text file can be just as useful. Here's a simple example:

```
Sub ExportToTextFile()
    Dim filePath As String
    Dim textLine As String
    Dim rowNumber As Integer

    filePath = "C:\path\to\your\output.txt" ' Specify your
output file path here
    rowNumber = 1 ' Start reading from the first row

    Open filePath For Output As #1 ' Open the text file
for writing

    Do While Cells(rowNumber, 1).Value <> "" ' Loop until
an empty cell is found
        textLine = Cells(rowNumber, 1).Value ' Read a cell
value
        Print #1, textLine ' Write the value to the text
file
        rowNumber = rowNumber + 1 ' Move to the next row
    Loop

    Close #1 ' Close the text file
End Sub
```

In this example:

- We open a text file for output.
- We read data from the first column of the Excel sheet and write each value to the text file.
- The loop stops when an empty cell is encountered.

Exporting data to another workbook

If you need to export data to another Excel workbook, here's how you can do it:

```
Sub ExportToWorkbook()
    Dim targetWorkbook As Workbook
    Dim targetSheet As Worksheet
    Dim sourceSheet As Worksheet
```

```
        ' Define the source and target workbooks and sheets
        Set sourceSheet = ThisWorkbook.Sheets("Sheet1")
        Set targetWorkbook = Workbooks.Add ' Create a new
workbook
        Set targetSheet = targetWorkbook.Sheets(1)

        ' Copy data from source to target
        sourceSheet.Range("A1:C10").Copy
Destination:=targetSheet.Range("A1")

        ' Save the target workbook
        targetWorkbook.SaveAs
"C:\path\to\your\targetWorkbook.xlsx"
        targetWorkbook.Close
    End Sub
```

In this example:

- We create a new workbook and specify the worksheet to copy to.
- We copy a range of data from the source worksheet to the target worksheet.
- We save and close the new workbook.

Putting it all together

Let's combine importing and exporting into a single macro. Imagine you have a text file with raw data and you need to clean it up and export it to a new workbook.

```
    Sub ImportCleanExport()
        Dim filePath As String
        Dim textLine As String
        Dim rowNumber As Integer
        Dim cleanedData As String

        filePath = "C:\path\to\your\rawData.txt"
        rowNumber = 1

        ' Step 1: Import Data
```

```
Open filePath For Input As #1

Do Until EOF(1)
    Line Input #1, textLine
    ' Clean data (e.g., trim spaces)
    cleanedData = Trim(textLine)
    Cells(rowNumber, 1).Value = cleanedData
    rowNumber = rowNumber + 1
Loop

Close #1

' Step 2: Export Cleaned Data
Dim targetWorkbook As Workbook
Dim targetSheet As Worksheet
Dim sourceSheet As Worksheet

Set sourceSheet = ThisWorkbook.Sheets("Sheet1")
Set targetWorkbook = Workbooks.Add
Set targetSheet = targetWorkbook.Sheets(1)

sourceSheet.Range("A1:A" & rowNumber - 1).Copy
Destination:=targetSheet.Range("A1")

targetWorkbook.SaveAs
"C:\path\to\your\cleanedData.xlsx"
targetWorkbook.Close
End Sub
```

In this macro:

- We import data from a text file, clean it, and store it in the first column.
- We then export the cleaned data to a new workbook.

By mastering these techniques, you can easily move data in and out of Excel, making your spreadsheets more dynamic and powerful. Keep practicing, and soon you'll be a data manipulation wizard!

Sorting and filtering data

Now that you've learned how to import and export data, let's move on to sorting and filtering data in Excel using VBA. Sorting helps you organize your data in a specific order, while filtering allows you to display only the data that meets certain criteria. These tasks can make your data analysis much more manageable

Sorting data

Sorting data in a range

Sorting data is straightforward with VBA. Let's start with sorting a simple range of data.

```vba
Sub SortData()
    Dim ws As Worksheet
    Set ws = ThisWorkbook.Sheets("Sheet1")

    ' Define the range to sort
    Dim sortRange As Range
    Set sortRange = ws.Range("A1:B10")

    ' Sort the data in ascending order by the first column
(A)
    sortRange.Sort Key1:=ws.Range("A1"),
Order1:=xlAscending, Header:=xlYes
    End Sub
```

In this example:

- We define the worksheet and the range to sort.
- We use the Sort method to sort the data in ascending order by the first column (A).

Sorting by multiple columns

You can also sort by multiple columns. Here's how:

```vba
Sub SortByMultipleColumns()
    Dim ws As Worksheet
    Set ws = ThisWorkbook.Sheets("Sheet1")
```

```
' Define the range to sort
Dim sortRange As Range
Set sortRange = ws.Range("A1:C10")

' Sort by the first column (A) and then by the second
column (B)
sortRange.Sort Key1:=ws.Range("A1"),
Order1:=xlAscending, _
                    Key2:=ws.Range("B1"),
Order2:=xlDescending, Header:=xlYes
End Sub
```

In this example:

- We sort the data first by the first column (A) in ascending order.
- Then we sort by the second column (B) in descending order.

Filtering data

Applying a simple filter

Filtering data allows you to display only the rows that meet certain criteria.

```
Sub ApplyFilter()
    Dim ws As Worksheet
    Set ws = ThisWorkbook.Sheets("Sheet1")

    ' Define the range to filter
    Dim filterRange As Range
    Set filterRange = ws.Range("A1:B10")

    ' Apply a filter to show only rows where the value in
column A is greater than 50
    filterRange.AutoFilter Field:=1, Criteria1:=">50"
End Sub
```

In this example:

- We define the worksheet and the range to filter.

- We apply an autofilter to show only rows where the value in the first column (A) is greater than 50.

Filtering with multiple criteria

You can apply filters with multiple criteria to fine-tune your data view.

```
Sub ApplyMultipleFilters()
    Dim ws As Worksheet
    Set ws = ThisWorkbook.Sheets("Sheet1")

    ' Define the range to filter
    Dim filterRange As Range
    Set filterRange = ws.Range("A1:C10")

    ' Apply filters to show rows where:
    ' Column A is greater than 50
    ' Column B contains the text "Passed"
    filterRange.AutoFilter Field:=1, Criteria1:=">50"
    filterRange.AutoFilter Field:=2, Criteria1:="Passed"
End Sub
```

In this example:

- We filter the data to show rows where the first column (A) is greater than 50.
- Additionally, we filter to show only rows where the second column (B) contains the text "Passed"

Clearing filters

Once you're done with filtering, you might want to clear the filters to see all your data again.

```
Sub ClearFilters()
    Dim ws As Worksheet
    Set ws = ThisWorkbook.Sheets("Sheet1")

    If ws.AutoFilterMode Then
        ws.AutoFilterMode = False ' Clear all filters
    End If
```

```
        End Sub
```

In this example:

- We check if any filters are applied using *AutoFilterMode*.
- If filters are active, we clear them by setting *AutoFilterMode* to *False*.

Putting It all together

Let's create a more complex example that combines sorting and filtering. Imagine you have a list of students with their scores, and you want to filter the list to show only students who passed (score >= 60) and then sort them by their names.

```
        Sub FilterAndSortStudents()
            Dim ws As Worksheet
            Set ws = ThisWorkbook.Sheets("Sheet1")

            ' Define the range to filter and sort
            Dim dataRange As Range
            Set dataRange = ws.Range("A1:C20") ' Assuming columns
        A for names, B for scores, C for status

            ' Apply filter to show only rows where the score is 60
        or above
            dataRange.AutoFilter Field:=2, Criteria1:=">=60"

            ' Sort the filtered data by names (column A)
            dataRange.Sort Key1:=ws.Range("A2"),
        Order1:=xlAscending, Header:=xlYes
            End Sub
```

In this macro:

- We apply a filter to show only students with scores 60 or above.
- We then sort the filtered data by the students' names in ascending order.

By mastering sorting and filtering with VBA, you can quickly organize and sift through large datasets, making your data analysis tasks much more efficient. Keep practicing these techniques, and you'll soon be handling data like a pro!

Data validation and cleaning

Data validation and cleaning are crucial steps in ensuring your data is accurate and ready for analysis. With VBA, you can automate these tasks to save time and reduce errors. Let's explore some techniques to validate and clean your data.

Data validation

Validating data entry

Data validation helps you ensure that the data entered into your spreadsheet meets certain criteria. For example, you might want to ensure that only numbers are entered into a specific range of cells.

```
Sub ValidateNumericEntry()
    Dim ws As Worksheet
    Set ws = ThisWorkbook.Sheets("Sheet1")

    ' Define the range to apply data validation
    Dim validationRange As Range
    Set validationRange = ws.Range("A1:A10")

    ' Clear any existing validation
    validationRange.Validation.Delete

    ' Apply numeric validation
    validationRange.Validation.Add
Type:=xlValidateWholeNumber, _

AlertStyle:=xlValidAlertStop, _
                            Operator:=xlBetween, _
                            Formula1:="1", _
                            Formula2:="100"
    validationRange.Validation.ErrorMessage = "Please
enter a whole number between 1 and 100."
    End Sub
```

In this example:

- We define the worksheet and the range to validate.
- We clear any existing validation rules.
- We apply a validation rule to ensure that only whole numbers between 1 and 100 can be entered.

Using a list for data validation

You can also use a list to restrict data entry to predefined values.

```
Sub ValidateWithList()
    Dim ws As Worksheet
    Set ws = ThisWorkbook.Sheets("Sheet1")

    ' Define the range to apply data validation
    Dim validationRange As Range
    Set validationRange = ws.Range("B1:B10")

    ' Clear any existing validation
    validationRange.Validation.Delete

    ' Apply list validation
    validationRange.Validation.Add Type:=xlValidateList, _

AlertStyle:=xlValidAlertStop, _

Formula1:="Option1,Option2,Option3"
    validationRange.Validation.ErrorMessage = "Please
select a value from the list."
    End Sub
```

In this example:

- We apply a list validation rule to ensure that only values from "Option1, Option2, Option3" can be entered into the specified range.

Data cleaning

Data cleaning involves removing or correcting incorrect, incomplete, or irrelevant data. Let's look at some common data cleaning tasks.

Removing duplicates

Duplicates can skew your data analysis. Here's how you can remove them using VBA:

```vba
Sub RemoveDuplicates()
    Dim ws As Worksheet
    Set ws = ThisWorkbook.Sheets("Sheet1")

    ' Define the range to remove duplicates from
    Dim dataRange As Range
    Set dataRange = ws.Range("A1:B10")

    ' Remove duplicates
    dataRange.RemoveDuplicates Columns:=Array(1, 2),
Header:=xlYes
End Sub
```

In this example:

- We specify the range from which to remove duplicates.
- The *RemoveDuplicates* method removes any duplicate rows based on the specified columns.

Trimming whitespace

Sometimes data entries have extra spaces that need to be removed. Here's how to trim those spaces:

```vba
Sub TrimWhitespace()
    Dim ws As Worksheet
    Set ws = ThisWorkbook.Sheets("Sheet1")

    Dim cell As Range

    ' Loop through each cell in the specified range and
trim whitespace
    For Each cell In ws.Range("A1:A10")
        If Not IsEmpty(cell.Value) Then
            cell.Value = Trim(cell.Value)
        End If
    Next cell
```

```
        End Sub
```
In this example:

- We loop through each cell in the specified range.
- The *Trim* function removes any leading or trailing spaces from the cell values.

Correcting case

Ensuring consistency in text case can make your data more uniform and easier to read.

```
Sub CorrectCase()
    Dim ws As Worksheet
    Set ws = ThisWorkbook.Sheets("Sheet1")

    Dim cell As Range

    ' Loop through each cell in the specified range and
convert text to proper case
    For Each cell In ws.Range("A1:A10")
        If Not IsEmpty(cell.Value) And IsText(cell.Value)
Then
            cell.Value =
Application.WorksheetFunction.Proper(cell.Value)
        End If
    Next cell
End Sub
```
In this example:

- We loop through each cell in the specified range.
- The **Proper** function converts text to proper case (i.e., the first letter of each word is capitalized).

Putting it all together

Let's create a macro that validates, cleans, and prepares data for analysis. This macro will:

- Ensure numeric entries are between 1 and 100.
- Remove duplicates.

- Trim whitespace.
- Correct the case of text entries.

```
Sub ValidateAndCleanData()
    Dim ws As Worksheet
    Set ws = ThisWorkbook.Sheets("Sheet1")

    ' Step 1: Validate numeric entries
    Dim validationRange As Range
    Set validationRange = ws.Range("A1:A10")
    validationRange.Validation.Delete
    validationRange.Validation.Add
Type:=xlValidateWholeNumber, _

AlertStyle:=xlValidAlertStop, _
                                Operator:=xlBetween, _
                                Formula1:="1", _
                                Formula2:="100"
    validationRange.Validation.ErrorMessage = "Please enter a
whole number between 1 and 100."

    ' Step 2: Remove duplicates
    Dim dataRange As Range
    Set dataRange = ws.Range("A1:B10")
    dataRange.RemoveDuplicates Columns:=Array(1, 2),
Header:=xlYes

    ' Step 3: Trim whitespace and correct case
    Dim cell As Range
    For Each cell In ws.Range("A1:A10")
        If Not IsEmpty(cell.Value) Then
            cell.Value = Trim(cell.Value)
            If IsText(cell.Value) Then
                cell.Value =
Application.WorksheetFunction.Proper(cell.Value)
            End If
```

```
        End If
    Next cell
End Sub
```

In this macro:

- We validate numeric entries to ensure they are within the range of 1 to 100.
- We remove duplicate rows based on the specified columns.
- We trim whitespace and correct the text case in the specified range.

By mastering data validation and cleaning with VBA, you can ensure your data is accurate and ready for any analysis, making your work more efficient and reliable. Keep practicing these techniques, and you'll be well on your way to becoming an Excel data management expert!

4. Working with ranges and cells

One of the most common tasks in Excel is working with ranges and cells. This includes selecting, copying, and pasting data, as well as using formulas within your VBA code. These operations form the foundation of many automated tasks in Excel.

Selecting, copying, and pasting ranges

Selecting ranges

Selecting a range is the first step for many operations in Excel. Here's how you can do it with VBA:

```
Sub SelectRange()
    Dim ws As Worksheet
    Set ws = ThisWorkbook.Sheets("Sheet1")

    ' Select the range A1 to B10
    ws.Range("A1:B10").Select
End Sub
```

In this example:

- We define the worksheet and select the range A1 to B10.

Copying and pasting ranges

Copying and pasting data between ranges is another essential operation. Let's look at a basic example:

```vba
Sub CopyAndPasteRange()
    Dim ws As Worksheet
    Set ws = ThisWorkbook.Sheets("Sheet1")

    ' Copy the range A1 to B10
    ws.Range("A1:B10").Copy

    ' Paste the copied range starting at cell D1
    ws.Range("D1").PasteSpecial Paste:=xlPasteAll
End Sub
```

In this example:

- We copy the range A1 to B10.
- We paste the copied data starting at cell D1 using the PasteSpecial method.

Copying and pasting values only

Sometimes, you might want to copy and paste only the values, without any formatting or formulas. Here's how:

```vba
Sub CopyAndPasteValues()
    Dim ws As Worksheet
    Set ws = ThisWorkbook.Sheets("Sheet1")

    ' Copy the range A1 to B10
    ws.Range("A1:B10").Copy

    ' Paste only the values starting at cell D1
    ws.Range("D1").PasteSpecial Paste:=xlPasteValues
End Sub
```

In this example:

- We copy the range A1 to B10.
- We paste only the values starting at cell D1 using *PasteSpecial* with the *xlPasteValues* option.

Using formulas in VBA

Using formulas in VBA allows you to automate complex calculations and data manipulations.

Inserting formulas

You can insert formulas into cells directly from VBA. Here's an example:

```
Sub InsertFormula()
    Dim ws As Worksheet
    Set ws = ThisWorkbook.Sheets("Sheet1")

    ' Insert a SUM formula into cell C1 to sum the range
A1 to A10
    ws.Range("C1").Formula = "=SUM(A1:A10)"
End Sub
```

In this example:

- We insert a SUM formula into cell C1 that sums the values in the range A1 to A10.

Using variables in formulas

You can also use variables within your formulas for more dynamic calculations.

```
Sub InsertDynamicFormula()
    Dim ws As Worksheet
    Set ws = ThisWorkbook.Sheets("Sheet1")

    Dim startRow As Integer
    Dim endRow As Integer

    startRow = 1
    endRow = 10

    ' Insert a SUM formula into cell C1 using variables
for the range
    ws.Range("C1").Formula = "=SUM(A" & startRow & ":A" &
endRow & ")"
```

```
    End Sub
```

In this example:

- We use variables *startRow* and *endRow* to define the range for the SUM formula.

Using the R1C1 notation

R1C1 notation is an alternative way to refer to cells and ranges. It can be very useful for relative references.

```
Sub InsertR1C1Formula()
    Dim ws As Worksheet
    Set ws = ThisWorkbook.Sheets("Sheet1")

    ' Insert a formula into cell C1 to sum the range A1 to
A10 using R1C1 notation
    ws.Range("C1").FormulaR1C1 = "=SUM(R1C1:R10C1)"
End Sub
```

In this example:

- We insert a SUM formula into cell C1 using R1C1 notation, which references the range from row 1, column 1 to row 10, column 1.

Putting it all together

Let's create a macro that combines selecting, copying, pasting, and using formulas. Suppose you want to copy data from one range, paste it to another location, and then insert a formula to sum a column.

```
Sub ManipulateData()
    Dim ws As Worksheet
    Set ws = ThisWorkbook.Sheets("Sheet1")

    ' Step 1: Select and copy the range A1 to B10
    ws.Range("A1:B10").Copy

    ' Step 2: Paste the copied range starting at cell D1
    ws.Range("D1").PasteSpecial Paste:=xlPasteAll
```

```
      ' Step 3: Insert a SUM formula into cell F1 to sum the
range D1 to D10
      ws.Range("F1").Formula = "=SUM(D1:D10)"

      ' Step 4: Clear the clipboard to free up memory
      Application.CutCopyMode = False
End Sub
```

In this macro:

- We copy the range A1 to B10.
- We paste the copied data starting at cell D1.
- We insert a SUM formula into cell F1 to sum the values in the range D1 to D10.
- We clear the clipboard to free up memory.

By mastering these techniques for working with ranges and cells, you can efficiently manipulate data and automate repetitive tasks in Excel. Keep practicing, and soon you'll be able to handle complex data operations with ease!

5. Creating custom functions

Custom functions, also known as user-defined functions (UDFs), are one of the most powerful features of VBA. They allow you to extend Excel's built-in functions with your own custom calculations and operations. Let's explore how to write UDFs and see some examples of useful functions for everyday tasks.

Writing user-defined functions (UDFs)

What is a UDF?

A UDF is a function that you create using VBA that can be used just like Excel's built-in functions. You can call these functions in your worksheets to perform custom calculations.

Creating your first UDF

Let's start by creating a simple UDF that adds two numbers together.

```
Function AddTwoNumbers(num1 As Double, num2 As Double) As
Double
      AddTwoNumbers = num1 + num2
```

```
End Function
```

In this example:

- *Function* keyword is used to declare the function.
- *AddTwoNumbers* is the name of the function.
- *num1* and *num2* are the input parameters.
- *As Double* specifies the data type of the input parameters and the return value.
- The function adds the two numbers and returns the result.

You can use this function in a worksheet by typing *=AddTwoNumbers(3, 5)* in a cell, and it will return *8*.

Examples of useful UDFs (e.g., string manipulation, date calculations)

Let's explore some practical UDFs that can help with common tasks like string manipulation and date calculations.

String manipulation

Concatenate strings

Concatenating strings can be very useful when dealing with text data.

```
Function ConcatenateStrings(text1 As String, text2 As
String) As String
    ConcatenateStrings = text1 & " " & text2
End Function
```

In this example:

- This function takes two strings as input and concatenates them with a space in between.
- You can use this function in a worksheet by typing *=ConcatenateStrings("Hello", "World")*, which will return *Hello World*.

Reverse a string

Reversing a string is another useful text manipulation function.

```
Function ReverseString(text As String) As String
    Dim i As Integer
    Dim reversedText As String
```

```
reversedText = ""
For i = Len(text) To 1 Step -1
    reversedText = reversedText & Mid(text, i, 1)
Next i

ReverseString = reversedText
End Function
```

In this example:

- This function takes a string as input and reverses its characters.
- You can use this function in a worksheet by typing =ReverseString("Excel"), which will return *lecxE*.

Date calculations

Days between dates

Calculating the number of days between two dates is a common requirement.

```
Function DaysBetween(startDate As Date, endDate As Date)
As Long
    DaysBetween = endDate - startDate
End Function
```

In this example:

- This function takes two dates as input and returns the number of days between them.
- You can use this function in a worksheet by typing =DaysBetween("2023-01-01", "2023-12-31"), which will return *364*.

Add business days

Adding business days (excluding weekends) to a date is useful for project planning.

```
Function AddBusinessDays(startDate As Date, days As Long)
As Date
    Dim currentDate As Date
    Dim addedDays As Long

    currentDate = startDate
```

```
addedDays = 0

Do While addedDays < days
    currentDate = currentDate + 1
    If Weekday(currentDate, vbMonday) <= 5 Then
        addedDays = addedDays + 1
    End If
Loop

AddBusinessDays = currentDate
End Function
```

In this example:

- This function takes a start date and the number of business days to add as input.
- It loops through each day, skipping weekends, until the required number of business days is added.
- You can use this function in a worksheet by typing *=AddBusinessDays("2023-01-01", 10)*, which will return the date 10 business days from January 1, 2023.

Putting it all together

Creating UDFs allows you to tailor Excel to your specific needs, making it an even more powerful tool. Here's a final example that combines string manipulation and date calculation:

```
Function FormatGreeting(name As String, birthDate As Date)
As String
    Dim age As Long
    Dim today As Date

    today = Date
    age = Year(today) - Year(birthDate)
    If Month(today) < Month(birthDate) Or (Month(today) =
Month(birthDate) And Day(today) < Day(birthDate)) Then
        age = age - 1
    End If
```

```
        FormatGreeting = "Hello " & name & "! You are " & age
& " years old."
End Function
```

In this example:

- This function takes a name and a birthdate as input.
- It calculates the age based on the current date.
- It returns a formatted greeting message.
- You can use this function in a worksheet by typing *=FormatGreeting("Alice", "1990-05-15")*, which will return something like *Hello Alice! You are 33 years old.*.

By mastering UDFs, you can create custom solutions tailored to your specific needs, making your Excel workbooks more powerful and efficient. Keep experimenting with different functions and soon you'll have a library of useful UDFs at your disposal!

6. Advanced data analysis

Excel's data analysis capabilities are robust, and with VBA, you can take these capabilities to the next level. This chapter will cover how to use PivotTables in VBA, automate chart creation, and generate automated reports. Let's dive in and see how you can streamline your data analysis tasks with VBA.

Using PivotTables in VBA

PivotTables are a powerful tool for summarizing and analyzing data. With VBA, you can create and manipulate PivotTables automatically, saving you a lot of time.

Creating a PivotTable

Let's start by creating a PivotTable from a dataset.

```
Sub CreatePivotTable()
    Dim wsData As Worksheet
    Dim wsPivot As Worksheet
    Dim pivotTableRange As Range
    Dim pivotTable As PivotTable
    Dim pivotCache As PivotCache
```

```
' Define the data and pivot table sheets
Set wsData = ThisWorkbook.Sheets("Data")
Set wsPivot = ThisWorkbook.Sheets("PivotTable")

' Define the range of data for the pivot table
Set pivotTableRange = wsData.Range("A1:C100")

' Create the pivot cache
Set pivotCache = ThisWorkbook.PivotCaches.Create( _
    SourceType:=xlDatabase, _
    SourceData:=pivotTableRange)

' Create the pivot table
Set pivotTable = pivotCache.CreatePivotTable( _
    TableDestination:=wsPivot.Range("A3"), _
    TableName:="MyPivotTable")

' Add fields to the pivot table
With pivotTable
    .PivotFields("Category").Orientation = xlRowField
    .PivotFields("Date").Orientation = xlColumnField
    .PivotFields("Sales").Orientation = xlDataField
    .PivotFields("Sales").Function = xlSum
End With
End Sub
```

In this example:

- We define the worksheets and the data range for the PivotTable.
- We create a pivot cache from the data range.
- We create the PivotTable in a specified location.
- We add fields to the PivotTable for rows, columns, and values.

Modifying an existing PivotTable

You can also modify an existing PivotTable. Let's add another field to the PivotTable created above.

```
Sub ModifyPivotTable()
```

```
        Dim wsPivot As Worksheet
        Dim pivotTable As PivotTable

        ' Define the pivot table sheet
        Set wsPivot = ThisWorkbook.Sheets("PivotTable")

        ' Get the pivot table
        Set pivotTable = wsPivot.PivotTables("MyPivotTable")

        ' Add another field to the pivot table
        With pivotTable
            .PivotFields("Region").Orientation = xlPageField
        End With
    End Sub
```

In this example:

- We reference the existing PivotTable by its name.
- We add a new field to the PivotTable as a page field (filter).

Automating chart creation

Charts are a great way to visualize data. With VBA, you can automate the creation of charts to dynamically represent your data.

Creating a Chart

Let's create a simple chart from a dataset.

```
    Sub CreateChart()
        Dim wsData As Worksheet
        Dim chartObject As ChartObject
        Dim chartRange As Range

        ' Define the data sheet
        Set wsData = ThisWorkbook.Sheets("Data")

        ' Define the range of data for the chart
        Set chartRange = wsData.Range("A1:B10")
```

```
        ' Add a new chart
        Set chartObject = wsData.ChartObjects.Add(Left:=100,
    Width:=375, Top:=50, Height:=225)

        ' Set the chart data source
        chartObject.Chart.SetSourceData Source:=chartRange

        ' Customize the chart
        With chartObject.Chart
            .ChartType = xlColumnClustered
            .HasTitle = True
            .ChartTitle.Text = "Sales Data"
            .Axes(xlCategory, xlPrimary).HasTitle = True
            .Axes(xlCategory, xlPrimary).AxisTitle.Text =
    "Date"
            .Axes(xlValue, xlPrimary).HasTitle = True
            .Axes(xlValue, xlPrimary).AxisTitle.Text = "Sales"
        End With
    End Sub
```

In this example:

- We define the worksheet and data range for the chart.
- We add a new chart to the worksheet.
- We set the data source for the chart and customize it by setting the chart type, title, and axis titles.

Generating automated reports

Automating report generation can save you a lot of time, especially if you need to produce regular reports with updated data.

Creating an automated report

Let's create a macro that generates a report by summarizing data, creating a PivotTable, and adding a chart.

```
        Sub GenerateReport()
            Dim wsData As Worksheet
            Dim wsReport As Worksheet
            Dim pivotTable As PivotTable
```

```vba
    Dim pivotCache As PivotCache
    Dim chartObject As ChartObject
    Dim reportRange As Range

    ' Define the data and report sheets
    Set wsData = ThisWorkbook.Sheets("Data")
    Set wsReport = ThisWorkbook.Sheets("Report")

    ' Clear any existing content in the report sheet
    wsReport.Cells.Clear

    ' Define the range of data for the pivot table
    Set reportRange = wsData.Range("A1:C100")

    ' Create the pivot cache
    Set pivotCache = ThisWorkbook.PivotCaches.Create( _
        SourceType:=xlDatabase, _
        SourceData:=reportRange)

    ' Create the pivot table
    Set pivotTable = pivotCache.CreatePivotTable( _
        TableDestination:=wsReport.Range("A3"), _
        TableName:="ReportPivotTable")

    ' Add fields to the pivot table
    With pivotTable
        .PivotFields("Category").Orientation = xlRowField
        .PivotFields("Date").Orientation = xlColumnField
        .PivotFields("Sales").Orientation = xlDataField
        .PivotFields("Sales").Function = xlSum
    End With

    ' Create a chart based on the pivot table
    Set chartObject = wsReport.ChartObjects.Add(Left:=300,
Width:=375, Top:=50, Height:=225)
```

```vba
        chartObject.Chart.SetSourceData
Source:=wsReport.Range("A3")

        ' Customize the chart
        With chartObject.Chart
            .ChartType = xlColumnClustered
            .HasTitle = True
            .ChartTitle.Text = "Sales Report"
            .Axes(xlCategory, xlPrimary).HasTitle = True
            .Axes(xlCategory, xlPrimary).AxisTitle.Text =
"Date"
            .Axes(xlValue, xlPrimary).HasTitle = True
            .Axes(xlValue, xlPrimary).AxisTitle.Text = "Sales"
        End With

        ' Add a title to the report sheet
        wsReport.Range("A1").Value = "Sales Report"
        wsReport.Range("A1").Font.Size = 16
        wsReport.Range("A1").Font.Bold = True
    End Sub
```

In this example:

- We define the worksheets and data range for the report.
- We clear any existing content in the report sheet to start fresh.
- We create a PivotTable to summarize the data.
- We create a chart based on the PivotTable.
- We customize the chart and add a title to the report.

By mastering these techniques for using PivotTables, automating chart creation, and generating automated reports, you can greatly enhance your data analysis capabilities in Excel. Keep practicing, and you'll soon be able to automate complex reporting tasks with ease!

Chapter 3: Automating Word tasks

Microsoft Word is a powerful tool for creating documents, and with VBA, you can automate many of the tasks you perform manually. This chapter will show you how to create and format documents, and how to insert text, images, and tables using VBA. Let's dive in!

7. Document automation

Creating and formatting documents

Creating a New Document

Creating a new Word document with VBA is simple. Here's how you can do it:

```
Sub CreateNewDocument()
    Dim wdApp As Object
    Dim wdDoc As Object

    ' Create a new instance of Word
    Set wdApp = CreateObject("Word.Application")

    ' Make Word visible
    wdApp.Visible = True

    ' Add a new document
    Set wdDoc = wdApp.Documents.Add

    ' Optional: Add a title to the document
    wdDoc.Content.Text = "My New Document"
    wdDoc.Paragraphs(1).Range.Font.Size = 24
    wdDoc.Paragraphs(1).Range.Font.Bold = True
End Sub
```

In this example:

- We create a new instance of Word and make it visible.
- We add a new document.

- We add a title to the document and format it with a larger font size and bold text.

Formatting text

Formatting text can be done easily with VBA. Here's an example:

```
Sub FormatText()
    Dim wdApp As Object
    Dim wdDoc As Object

    ' Create a new instance of Word
    Set wdApp = CreateObject("Word.Application")
    wdApp.Visible = True

    ' Add a new document
    Set wdDoc = wdApp.Documents.Add

    ' Add some text
    wdDoc.Content.Text = "This is a sample paragraph."

    ' Format the text
    With wdDoc.Paragraphs(1).Range
        .Font.Name = "Arial"
        .Font.Size = 12
        .Font.Color = RGB(255, 0, 0) ' Red color
        .ParagraphFormat.Alignment = 1 ' Center alignment
    End With
End Sub
```

In this example:

- We create a new Word document and add some text.
- We format the text by setting the font name, size, color, and alignment.

Inserting text, images, and tables

Inserting Text

Inserting text at specific locations in a document is straightforward. Here's how:

```
Sub InsertText()
    Dim wdApp As Object
    Dim wdDoc As Object

    ' Create a new instance of Word
    Set wdApp = CreateObject("Word.Application")
    wdApp.Visible = True

    ' Add a new document
    Set wdDoc = wdApp.Documents.Add

    ' Insert text at the beginning of the document
    wdDoc.Content.InsertBefore "This is the beginning of
the document." & vbCrLf

    ' Insert text at the end of the document
    wdDoc.Content.InsertAfter vbCrLf & "This is the end of
the document."
    End Sub
```

In this example:

- We insert text at the beginning and end of the document using *InsertBefore* and *InsertAfter*.

Inserting images

Inserting images into a Word document can enhance its visual appeal. Here's how to do it with VBA:

```
Sub InsertImage()
    Dim wdApp As Object
    Dim wdDoc As Object
    Dim imagePath As String

    ' Path to the image
    imagePath = "C:\path\to\your\image.jpg"
```

```vba
    ' Create a new instance of Word
    Set wdApp = CreateObject("Word.Application")
    wdApp.Visible = True

    ' Add a new document
    Set wdDoc = wdApp.Documents.Add

    ' Insert the image
    wdDoc.InlineShapes.AddPicture FileName:=imagePath,
LinkToFile:=False, SaveWithDocument:=True
    End Sub
```

In this example:

- We specify the path to the image and insert it into the document using *AddPicture*.

Inserting tables

Tables are useful for organizing data in a document. Here's how to insert and format a table with VBA:

```vba
Sub InsertTable()
    Dim wdApp As Object
    Dim wdDoc As Object
    Dim wdTable As Object

    ' Create a new instance of Word
    Set wdApp = CreateObject("Word.Application")
    wdApp.Visible = True

    ' Add a new document
    Set wdDoc = wdApp.Documents.Add

    ' Insert a table with 3 rows and 4 columns
    Set wdTable = wdDoc.Tables.Add(Range:=wdDoc.Content,
NumRows:=3, NumColumns:=4)

    ' Fill in the table with some data
```

```
wdTable.Cell(1, 1).Range.Text = "Header 1"
wdTable.Cell(1, 2).Range.Text = "Header 2"
wdTable.Cell(1, 3).Range.Text = "Header 3"
wdTable.Cell(1, 4).Range.Text = "Header 4"
wdTable.Cell(2, 1).Range.Text = "Data 1"
wdTable.Cell(2, 2).Range.Text = "Data 2"
wdTable.Cell(2, 3).Range.Text = "Data 3"
wdTable.Cell(2, 4).Range.Text = "Data 4"

' Format the table
With wdTable
    .Rows(1).Range.Font.Bold = True
    .Borders.Enable = True
    .Rows.SetHeight RowHeight:=20,
HeightRule:=wdRowHeightExactly
    End With
End Sub
```

In this example:

- We insert a table with 3 rows and 4 columns.
- We fill the table with data.
- We format the table by making the first row bold, enabling borders, and setting the row height.

Putting it all together

Let's create a macro that combines creating a new document, inserting text, images, and tables, and formatting them. This will give you a comprehensive example of document automation in Word.

```
Sub CreateAndFormatDocument()
    Dim wdApp As Object
    Dim wdDoc As Object
    Dim wdTable As Object
    Dim imagePath As String

    ' Path to the image
    imagePath = "C:\path\to\your\image.jpg"
```

```vba
' Create a new instance of Word
Set wdApp = CreateObject("Word.Application")
wdApp.Visible = True

' Add a new document
Set wdDoc = wdApp.Documents.Add

' Insert a title
wdDoc.Content.InsertBefore "Automated Document" &
vbCrLf
With wdDoc.Paragraphs(1).Range
    .Font.Size = 24
    .Font.Bold = True
    .ParagraphFormat.Alignment = 1 ' Center alignment
End With

' Insert an introductory paragraph
wdDoc.Content.InsertAfter vbCrLf & "This document was
created and formatted using VBA." & vbCrLf

' Insert an image
wdDoc.Content.InsertAfter vbCrLf & "Here is an example
image:" & vbCrLf
wdDoc.InlineShapes.AddPicture FileName:=imagePath,
LinkToFile:=False, SaveWithDocument:=True

' Insert a table
wdDoc.Content.InsertAfter vbCrLf & "Here is an example
table:" & vbCrLf
Set wdTable = wdDoc.Tables.Add(Range:=wdDoc.Content,
NumRows:=3, NumColumns:=4)
wdTable.Cell(1, 1).Range.Text = "Header 1"
wdTable.Cell(1, 2).Range.Text = "Header 2"
wdTable.Cell(1, 3).Range.Text = "Header 3"
wdTable.Cell(1, 4).Range.Text = "Header 4"
wdTable.Cell(2, 1).Range.Text = "Data 1"
```

```
        wdTable.Cell(2, 2).Range.Text = "Data 2"
        wdTable.Cell(2, 3).Range.Text = "Data 3"
        wdTable.Cell(2, 4).Range.Text = "Data 4"


        ' Format the table
        With wdTable
            .Rows(1).Range.Font.Bold = True
            .Borders.Enable = True
            .Rows.SetHeight RowHeight:=20,
    HeightRule:=wdRowHeightExactly
        End With


        ' Add a closing paragraph
        wdDoc.Content.InsertAfter vbCrLf & "This is the end of
    the automated document."
        With wdDoc.Paragraphs.Last.Range
            .Font.Italic = True
            .ParagraphFormat.Alignment = 2 ' Right alignment
        End With
    End Sub
```

In this comprehensive example:

- We create a new Word document and add a formatted title.
- We insert an introductory paragraph, an image, and a table with data.
- We format the table and add a closing paragraph.

By mastering these techniques, you can automate the creation and formatting of Word documents, making your document management tasks more efficient and consistent. Keep practicing, and soon you'll be able to create complex documents with ease!

8. Mail merge automation

Mail merge is a powerful feature in Microsoft Word that allows you to create personalized documents like letters, labels, and emails by merging a Word template with data from an Excel spreadsheet. Automating this process with VBA can save you a lot of time, especially when dealing with large datasets. In this chapter, we'll cover how to automate mail merge from Excel data and how to customize mail merge templates.

Automating mail merge from Excel data

Setting up your Excel data

Before you start the mail merge process, ensure your Excel data is well-organized. Typically, this involves having a header row with column names and subsequent rows with the data to be merged. For example, your Excel file might look like this:

	A	B	C	D	E	F
1	FirstName	LastName	Address	City	State	Zip
2	John	Doe	123 Elm St.	Anytown	CA	12345
3	Jane	Smith	456 Oak St.	Othertown	NY	67890

Automating mail merge

Here's a VBA script to automate the mail merge process using data from an Excel file:

```
Sub AutomateMailMerge()
    Dim wdApp As Object
    Dim wdDoc As Object
    Dim excelFilePath As String
    Dim mailMergeTemplate As String

    ' Path to the Excel file
    excelFilePath = "C:\path\to\your\ExcelData.xlsx"

    ' Path to the Word mail merge template
    mailMergeTemplate =
"C:\path\to\your\MailMergeTemplate.docx"

    ' Create a new instance of Word
    Set wdApp = CreateObject("Word.Application")
    wdApp.Visible = True

    ' Open the mail merge template
    Set wdDoc = wdApp.Documents.Open(mailMergeTemplate)
```

```
        ' Set up the mail merge
        With wdDoc.MailMerge
            .MainDocumentType = wdFormLetters
            .OpenDataSource Name:=excelFilePath, _
                            ReadOnly:=True, _
                            AddToRecentFiles:=False, _
                            Revert:=False, _
                            Format:=wdOpenFormatAuto, _

    Connection:="Provider=Microsoft.ACE.OLEDB.12.0;User
    ID=Admin;Data Source=" & excelFilePath &
    ";Mode=Read;Extended Properties=""HDR=YES;IMEX=1"";", _
                            SQLStatement:="SELECT * FROM
    [Sheet1$]"

            ' Execute the mail merge
            .Destination = wdSendToNewDocument
            .Execute Pause:=False
        End With

        ' Save the merged document
        wdApp.ActiveDocument.SaveAs2
    "C:\path\to\your\MergedDocument.docx"

        ' Close the mail merge template without saving
        wdDoc.Close SaveChanges:=False

        ' Optional: Close Word application
        ' wdApp.Quit
    End Sub
```

In this example:

- We specify the paths to the Excel file and the Word mail merge template.
- We create a new instance of Word and open the mail merge template.

- We set up the mail merge by connecting to the Excel data source and executing the merge.
- The merged document is saved to a specified location, and the template is closed without saving changes.

Customizing mail merge templates

Creating a mail merge template

To create a mail merge template in Word:

1. Open a new or existing Word document.

2. Go to the *Mailings* tab and click *Start Mail Merge*, then select *Letters* (or another document type).

3. Click *Select Recipients* and choose *Use an Existing List*.

4. Navigate to your Excel file and select it as the data source.

5. Insert merge fields by clicking *Insert Merge Field* and selecting the fields you want to use.

Example of a mail merge template

Here's an example of what your mail merge template might look like:

Dear «FirstName» «LastName»,

We are pleased to inform you that your address is recorded as:
«Address»
«City», «State» «Zip»

Thank you for your continued support.

Best regards,
Your Company Name

Customizing the template with VBA

You can further customize your mail merge templates using VBA. For example, you might want to conditionally format parts of your document or insert additional content dynamically.

```vba
Sub CustomizeMailMergeTemplate()
    Dim wdApp As Object
    Dim wdDoc As Object
    Dim mergeField As Object

    ' Path to the mail merge template
    Dim mailMergeTemplate As String
    mailMergeTemplate =
"C:\path\to\your\MailMergeTemplate.docx"

    ' Create a new instance of Word
    Set wdApp = CreateObject("Word.Application")
    wdApp.Visible = True

    ' Open the mail merge template
    Set wdDoc = wdApp.Documents.Open(mailMergeTemplate)

    ' Example: Add conditional text based on the content
of a merge field
    For Each mergeField In wdDoc.MailMerge.Fields
        If mergeField.Code.Text = " MERGEFIELD State "
Then
            mergeField.Select
            wdApp.Selection.TypeText Text:=" is located in
a beautiful region."
        End If
    Next mergeField

    ' Save the customized template
    wdDoc.SaveAs2
"C:\path\to\your\CustomizedMailMergeTemplate.docx"

    ' Close Word application
    wdApp.Quit
End Sub
```
In this example:

- We open the mail merge template.
- We loop through the merge fields to find a specific field (State) and add conditional text based on its content.
- We save the customized template.

By mastering mail merge automation and customizing templates with VBA, you can streamline the process of creating personalized documents, saving time and reducing errors.

9. Template management

Managing document templates efficiently can significantly streamline your workflow, especially if you frequently create similar types of documents. In this chapter, we will explore how to create and use document templates, as well as how to automate template updates using VBA.

Creating and using document templates

What is a template?

A template is a pre-designed document that you can use as a starting point for new documents. Templates contain formatting, styles, text, and other elements that you want to include in every document you create from that template.

Creating a template

Creating a template is straightforward. Here's how to do it:

1. **Open a new document:** Start by opening a new document in Word.

2. **Design your template:** Add all the elements you want to include in your template. This could be headers, footers, text styles, placeholder text, images, etc.

3. **Save as a template:** Save the document as a template file. Go to File > Save As. In the Save as type dropdown, select Word Template (*.dotx) and give your template a name.

Using a template

To use a template to create a new document:

1. **Open Word:** Open Word and go to File > New.

2. **Choose your template:** You can choose from the available templates, including any custom templates you've created. Click on your template to create a new document based on it.

Example: basic template creation

Here's an example of creating a simple template with a header, footer, and some placeholder text:

```vba
Sub CreateBasicTemplate()
    Dim wdApp As Object
    Dim wdDoc As Object

    ' Create a new instance of Word
    Set wdApp = CreateObject("Word.Application")
    wdApp.Visible = True

    ' Add a new document
    Set wdDoc = wdApp.Documents.Add

    ' Add header
    With
wdDoc.Sections(1).Headers(wdHeaderFooterPrimary).Range
        .Text = "Company Name"
        .Font.Size = 16
        .Font.Bold = True
        .ParagraphFormat.Alignment =
wdAlignParagraphCenter
    End With

    ' Add footer
    With
wdDoc.Sections(1).Footers(wdHeaderFooterPrimary).Range
        .Text = "Confidential"
        .Font.Size = 10
        .Font.Italic = True
        .ParagraphFormat.Alignment =
wdAlignParagraphCenter
```

```
                End With

            ' Add placeholder text
            wdDoc.Content.Text = "Dear [Recipient Name]," & vbCrLf
        & vbCrLf & _

                            "Thank you for your business." &
        vbCrLf & vbCrLf & _

                            "Sincerely," & vbCrLf & _
                            "[Your Name]"

            ' Save the document as a template
            wdDoc.SaveAs2 "C:\path\to\your\BasicTemplate.dotx",
        FileFormat:=wdFormatXMLTemplate

            ' Close the document
            wdDoc.Close SaveChanges:=False

            ' Optional: Close Word application
            ' wdApp.Quit
        End Sub
```

In this example:

- We create a new Word document.
- We add a header, footer, and placeholder text.
- We save the document as a template file.

Automating template updates

As your business or requirements change, you might need to update your templates. Automating this process ensures consistency and saves time.

Updating a template

Let's say you need to update the header text in your template. Here's how to do it with VBA:

```
        Sub UpdateTemplateHeader()
            Dim wdApp As Object
            Dim wdDoc As Object
```

```
Dim templatePath As String

' Path to the template
templatePath = "C:\path\to\your\BasicTemplate.dotx"

' Create a new instance of Word
Set wdApp = CreateObject("Word.Application")
wdApp.Visible = True

' Open the template
Set wdDoc = wdApp.Documents.Open(templatePath)

' Update the header
With
wdDoc.Sections(1).Headers(wdHeaderFooterPrimary).Range
        .Text = "Updated Company Name"
        .Font.Size = 16
        .Font.Bold = True
        .ParagraphFormat.Alignment =
wdAlignParagraphCenter
    End With

' Save the updated template
wdDoc.Save

' Close the document
wdDoc.Close SaveChanges:=False

' Optional: Close Word application
' wdApp.Quit
    End Sub
```

In this example:

- We open the existing template.
- We update the header text.
- We save the changes to the template.

Updating multiple templates

If you have multiple templates that need the same update, you can automate this process for all of them. Here's an example of how to do it:

```vba
Sub UpdateMultipleTemplates()
    Dim wdApp As Object
    Dim wdDoc As Object
    Dim templatePaths As Variant
    Dim templatePath As Variant

    ' List of template paths
    templatePaths =
Array("C:\path\to\your\Template1.dotx", _

"C:\path\to\your\Template2.dotx", _

"C:\path\to\your\Template3.dotx")

    ' Create a new instance of Word
    Set wdApp = CreateObject("Word.Application")
    wdApp.Visible = True

    ' Loop through each template and update the header
    For Each templatePath In templatePaths
        Set wdDoc = wdApp.Documents.Open(templatePath)

        ' Update the header
        With
wdDoc.Sections(1).Headers(wdHeaderFooterPrimary).Range
            .Text = "Updated Company Name"
            .Font.Size = 16
            .Font.Bold = True
            .ParagraphFormat.Alignment =
wdAlignParagraphCenter
        End With
```

```
        ' Save the updated template
        wdDoc.Save
        wdDoc.Close SaveChanges:=False
    Next templatePath


        ' Optional: Close Word application
        ' wdApp.Quit
    End Sub
```

In this example:

- We specify an array of template paths.
- We loop through each template, open it, update the header, and save the changes.

By mastering template management and automation, you can ensure consistency across your documents and save a significant amount of time. Keep practicing these techniques to enhance your efficiency and productivity!

Chapter 4: Automating PowerPoint tasks

10. Slide creation and formatting

PowerPoint is a powerful tool for creating presentations, and with VBA, you can automate the creation and formatting of slides. This chapter will show you how to automate slide creation and format slides and objects efficiently. Let's get started!

Automating slide creation

Creating a new presentation

First, let's create a new PowerPoint presentation and add some slides to it.

```
Sub CreateNewPresentation()
    Dim pptApp As Object
    Dim pptPresentation As Object
```

```
Dim slide1 As Object
Dim slide2 As Object

' Create a new instance of PowerPoint
Set pptApp = CreateObject("PowerPoint.Application")
pptApp.Visible = True

' Add a new presentation
Set pptPresentation = pptApp.Presentations.Add

' Add a title slide
Set slide1 = pptPresentation.Slides.Add(1, 1) ' 1 for
ppLayoutTitle
slide1.Shapes.Title.TextFrame.TextRange.Text = "Welcome to Our
Presentation"
slide1.Shapes.Placeholders(2).TextFrame.TextRange.Text =
"Subtitle goes here"

' Add a content slide
Set slide2 = pptPresentation.Slides.Add(2, 2) ' 2 for
ppLayoutText
slide2.Shapes.Title.TextFrame.TextRange.Text = "Agenda"
slide2.Shapes.Placeholders(2).TextFrame.TextRange.Text = "1.
Introduction" & vbCrLf & "2. Main Topic" & vbCrLf & "3.
Conclusion"
End Sub
```

In this example:

- We create a new instance of PowerPoint and make it visible.
- We add a new presentation.
- We add a title slide and a content slide with text.

Adding multiple slides

You can also automate the addition of multiple slides based on an array of titles and content.

```
Sub AddMultipleSlides()
    Dim pptApp As Object
```

```
Dim pptPresentation As Object
Dim slide As Object
Dim slideIndex As Integer
Dim titles As Variant
Dim contents As Variant
Dim i As Integer

' Array of slide titles and content
titles = Array("Introduction", "Main Topic",
"Conclusion")
contents = Array("Welcome to the introduction.", "Here
we discuss the main topic.", "Finally, we conclude.")

' Create a new instance of PowerPoint
Set pptApp = CreateObject("PowerPoint.Application")
pptApp.Visible = True

' Add a new presentation
Set pptPresentation = pptApp.Presentations.Add

' Loop through titles and contents to add slides
For i = LBound(titles) To UBound(titles)
    slideIndex = i + 1
    Set slide = pptPresentation.Slides.Add(slideIndex,
2) ' 2 for ppLayoutText
        slide.Shapes.Title.TextFrame.TextRange.Text =
titles(i)

slide.Shapes.Placeholders(2).TextFrame.TextRange.Text =
contents(i)
    Next i
End Sub
```

In this example:

- We define arrays of slide titles and content.
- We loop through these arrays to add slides dynamically.

Formatting slides and objects

Formatting text in slides

You can format text within slides to match your desired style.

```vba
Sub FormatSlideText()
    Dim pptApp As Object
    Dim pptPresentation As Object
    Dim slide As Object
    Dim textBox As Object

    ' Create a new instance of PowerPoint
    Set pptApp = CreateObject("PowerPoint.Application")
    pptApp.Visible = True

    ' Add a new presentation
    Set pptPresentation = pptApp.Presentations.Add

    ' Add a slide
    Set slide = pptPresentation.Slides.Add(1, 1) ' 1 for
ppLayoutTitle

    ' Add a text box and format the text
    Set textBox = slide.Shapes.AddTextbox(1, 100, 100,
500, 50) ' 1 for msoTextOrientationHorizontal
    textBox.TextFrame.TextRange.Text = "This is a
formatted text box."
    With textBox.TextFrame.TextRange
        .Font.Name = "Arial"
        .Font.Size = 24
        .Font.Bold = True
        .Font.Color = RGB(255, 0, 0) ' Red color
    End With
End Sub
```

In this example:

- We add a text box to a slide and format the text with specific font properties.

Formatting shapes

Formatting shapes can make your slides more visually appealing.

```
Sub FormatSlideShapes()
    Dim pptApp As Object
    Dim pptPresentation As Object
    Dim slide As Object
    Dim shape As Object

    ' Create a new instance of PowerPoint
    Set pptApp = CreateObject("PowerPoint.Application")
    pptApp.Visible = True

    ' Add a new presentation
    Set pptPresentation = pptApp.Presentations.Add

    ' Add a slide
    Set slide = pptPresentation.Slides.Add(1, 1) ' 1 for
ppLayoutTitle

    ' Add a rectangle shape and format it
    Set shape = slide.Shapes.AddShape(1, 100, 150, 300,
100) ' 1 for msoShapeRectangle
    shape.Fill.ForeColor.RGB = RGB(0, 255, 0) ' Green fill
    shape.Line.ForeColor.RGB = RGB(0, 0, 0) ' Black border
    shape.TextFrame.TextRange.Text = "Formatted Rectangle"
    shape.TextFrame.TextRange.Font.Size = 20
    shape.TextFrame.TextRange.Font.Bold = True
End Sub
```

In this example:

- We add a rectangle shape to a slide and format its fill color, border color, and text properties.

Putting it all together

Let's create a comprehensive example that combines slide creation and formatting. We'll create a presentation with multiple slides, formatted text, and shapes.

```
Sub CreateAndFormatPresentation()
    Dim pptApp As Object
    Dim pptPresentation As Object
    Dim slide As Object
    Dim textBox As Object
    Dim shape As Object
    Dim slideIndex As Integer
    Dim titles As Variant
    Dim contents As Variant
    Dim i As Integer

    ' Array of slide titles and content
    titles = Array("Introduction", "Main Topic",
"Conclusion")
    contents = Array("Welcome to the introduction.", "Here
we discuss the main topic.", "Finally, we conclude.")

    ' Create a new instance of PowerPoint
    Set pptApp = CreateObject("PowerPoint.Application")
    pptApp.Visible = True

    ' Add a new presentation
    Set pptPresentation = pptApp.Presentations.Add

    ' Loop through titles and contents to add and format
slides
    For i = LBound(titles) To UBound(titles)
        slideIndex = i + 1
        Set slide = pptPresentation.Slides.Add(slideIndex,
2) ' 2 for ppLayoutText
        slide.Shapes.Title.TextFrame.TextRange.Text =
titles(i)
```

```vba
slide.Shapes.Placeholders(2).TextFrame.TextRange.Text =
contents(i)

        ' Add and format a text box
        Set textBox = slide.Shapes.AddTextbox(1, 100, 300,
500, 50) ' 1 for msoTextOrientationHorizontal
        textBox.TextFrame.TextRange.Text = "This is slide
" & slideIndex
        With textBox.TextFrame.TextRange
            .Font.Name = "Arial"
            .Font.Size = 18
            .Font.Bold = True
            .Font.Color = RGB(0, 0, 255) ' Blue color
        End With

        ' Add and format a rectangle shape
        Set shape = slide.Shapes.AddShape(1, 100, 400,
300, 100) ' 1 for msoShapeRectangle
        shape.Fill.ForeColor.RGB = RGB(255, 255, 0) '
Yellow fill
        shape.Line.ForeColor.RGB = RGB(0, 0, 0) ' Black
border
        shape.TextFrame.TextRange.Text = "Formatted
Rectangle"
        shape.TextFrame.TextRange.Font.Size = 16
        shape.TextFrame.TextRange.Font.Bold = True
    Next i
    End Sub
```

In this comprehensive example:

- We create a new PowerPoint presentation.
- We loop through arrays of titles and content to add multiple slides.
- We add and format a text box and a rectangle shape on each slide.

By mastering these techniques for automating slide creation and formatting in PowerPoint, you can create dynamic and visually appealing presentations quickly and efficiently. Keep practicing, and soon you'll be able to automate even the most complex presentation tasks with ease!

11. Integrating data from Excel

PowerPoint presentations often need data from Excel to create compelling visuals. With VBA, you can embed charts and tables from Excel directly into your PowerPoint slides and ensure that this data stays updated automatically. In this chapter, we'll explore how to embed charts and tables from Excel and update linked data automatically.

Embedding charts and tables from Excel

Embedding a chart from Excel

Let's start by embedding a chart from an Excel workbook into a PowerPoint slide.

```vba
Sub EmbedChartFromExcel()
    Dim pptApp As Object
    Dim pptPresentation As Object
    Dim pptSlide As Object
    Dim excelApp As Object
    Dim excelWorkbook As Object
    Dim excelChart As Object

    ' Paths to the files
    Dim excelFilePath As String
    excelFilePath = "C:\path\to\your\ExcelFile.xlsx"

    ' Create a new instance of PowerPoint
    Set pptApp = CreateObject("PowerPoint.Application")
    pptApp.Visible = True

    ' Add a new presentation
    Set pptPresentation = pptApp.Presentations.Add

    ' Add a new slide
```

```
        Set pptSlide = pptPresentation.Slides.Add(1, 1) ' 1
for ppLayoutTitle

        ' Create a new instance of Excel and open the workbook
        Set excelApp = CreateObject("Excel.Application")
        Set excelWorkbook =
excelApp.Workbooks.Open(excelFilePath)

        ' Get the chart object from Excel (assuming the chart
is the first one in the workbook)
        Set excelChart =
excelWorkbook.Sheets("Sheet1").ChartObjects(1).Chart

        ' Copy the chart from Excel
        excelChart.ChartArea.Copy

        ' Paste the chart into the PowerPoint slide
        pptSlide.Shapes.PasteSpecial DataType:=10 ' 10 for
ppPasteEnhancedMetafile

        ' Clean up
        excelWorkbook.Close SaveChanges:=False
        excelApp.Quit
        Set excelChart = Nothing
        Set excelWorkbook = Nothing
        Set excelApp = Nothing
    End Sub
```

In this example:

- We open an Excel workbook and select a chart.
- We copy the chart and paste it into a PowerPoint slide as an enhanced metafile.

Embedding a table from Excel

Similarly, you can embed a table from Excel into a PowerPoint slide.

```
    Sub EmbedTableFromExcel()
        Dim pptApp As Object
```

```vba
    Dim pptPresentation As Object
    Dim pptSlide As Object
    Dim excelApp As Object
    Dim excelWorkbook As Object
    Dim tableRange As Range

    ' Paths to the files
    Dim excelFilePath As String
    excelFilePath = "C:\path\to\your\ExcelFile.xlsx"

    ' Create a new instance of PowerPoint
    Set pptApp = CreateObject("PowerPoint.Application")
    pptApp.Visible = True

    ' Add a new presentation
    Set pptPresentation = pptApp.Presentations.Add

    ' Add a new slide
    Set pptSlide = pptPresentation.Slides.Add(1, 1) ' 1
for ppLayoutTitle

    ' Create a new instance of Excel and open the workbook
    Set excelApp = CreateObject("Excel.Application")
    Set excelWorkbook =
excelApp.Workbooks.Open(excelFilePath)

    ' Define the range to copy (assuming the table is in
range A1:C10)
    Set tableRange =
excelWorkbook.Sheets("Sheet1").Range("A1:C10")

    ' Copy the table from Excel
    tableRange.Copy

    ' Paste the table into the PowerPoint slide
```

```
        pptSlide.Shapes.PasteSpecial DataType:=0 ' 0 for
ppPasteDefault

    ' Clean up
    excelWorkbook.Close SaveChanges:=False
    excelApp.Quit
    Set tableRange = Nothing
    Set excelWorkbook = Nothing
    Set excelApp = Nothing
End Sub
```

In this example:

- We define a range in Excel that contains the table.
- We copy the table and paste it into a PowerPoint slide.

Updating linked data automatically

Linking data between Excel and PowerPoint ensures that your presentation always shows the latest information. Let's look at how to update linked data automatically.

Linking a chart from Excel

First, let's link a chart from Excel so that it updates automatically when the data changes.

```
Sub LinkChartFromExcel()
    Dim pptApp As Object
    Dim pptPresentation As Object
    Dim pptSlide As Object
    Dim excelApp As Object
    Dim excelWorkbook As Object
    Dim excelChart As Object

    ' Paths to the files
    Dim excelFilePath As String
    excelFilePath = "C:\path\to\your\ExcelFile.xlsx"

    ' Create a new instance of PowerPoint
```

```
Set pptApp = CreateObject("PowerPoint.Application")
pptApp.Visible = True

' Add a new presentation
Set pptPresentation = pptApp.Presentations.Add

' Add a new slide
Set pptSlide = pptPresentation.Slides.Add(1, 1) ' 1
for ppLayoutTitle

' Create a new instance of Excel and open the workbook
Set excelApp = CreateObject("Excel.Application")
Set excelWorkbook =
excelApp.Workbooks.Open(excelFilePath)

' Get the chart object from Excel (assuming the chart
is the first one in the workbook)
Set excelChart =
excelWorkbook.Sheets("Sheet1").ChartObjects(1).Chart

' Copy the chart from Excel as a link
excelChart.ChartArea.Copy

' Paste the chart link into the PowerPoint slide
pptSlide.Shapes.PasteSpecial DataType:=5 ' 5 for
ppPasteOLEObject

' Clean up
excelWorkbook.Close SaveChanges:=False
excelApp.Quit
Set excelChart = Nothing
Set excelWorkbook = Nothing
Set excelApp = Nothing
End Sub
```

In this example:

- We copy the chart from Excel as a linked OLE object.
- We paste the linked chart into a PowerPoint slide, ensuring it updates automatically when the data changes.

Updating linked data

To update the linked data in your PowerPoint presentation, you can use VBA to refresh the links.

```
Sub UpdateLinkedData()
    Dim pptApp As Object
    Dim pptPresentation As Object
    Dim pptSlide As Object
    Dim shape As Object

    ' Create a new instance of PowerPoint
    Set pptApp = CreateObject("PowerPoint.Application")
    pptApp.Visible = True

    ' Open the presentation
    Set pptPresentation =
pptApp.Presentations.Open("C:\path\to\your\Presentation.pp
tx")

    ' Loop through each slide and update links
    For Each pptSlide In pptPresentation.Slides
        For Each shape In pptSlide.Shapes
            If shape.Type = 12 Then ' 12 for
msoLinkedOLEObject
                shape.LinkFormat.Update
            End If
        Next shape
    Next pptSlide
End Sub
```

In this example:

- We open an existing PowerPoint presentation.
- We loop through each slide and each shape on the slide.

- If a shape is a linked OLE object, we update the link to refresh the data.

Putting it all together

Let's create a comprehensive example that combines embedding and linking data from Excel into PowerPoint and updating the links automatically.

```
Sub IntegrateExcelData()
    Dim pptApp As Object
    Dim pptPresentation As Object
    Dim pptSlide As Object
    Dim excelApp As Object
    Dim excelWorkbook As Object
    Dim excelChart As Object
    Dim tableRange As Range

    ' Paths to the files
    Dim excelFilePath As String
    Dim presentationPath As String
    excelFilePath = "C:\path\to\your\ExcelFile.xlsx"
    presentationPath = "C:\path\to\your\Presentation.pptx"

    ' Create a new instance of PowerPoint
    Set pptApp = CreateObject("PowerPoint.Application")
    pptApp.Visible = True

    ' Add a new presentation
    Set pptPresentation = pptApp.Presentations.Add

    ' Add a new slide
    Set pptSlide = pptPresentation.Slides.Add(1, 1) ' 1
for ppLayoutTitle

    ' Create a new instance of Excel and open the workbook
    Set excelApp = CreateObject("Excel.Application")
    Set excelWorkbook =
excelApp.Workbooks.Open(excelFilePath)
```

```vba
' Get the chart object from Excel
Set excelChart =
excelWorkbook.Sheets("Sheet1").ChartObjects(1).Chart

' Copy and paste the chart as a linked object
excelChart.ChartArea.Copy
pptSlide.Shapes.PasteSpecial DataType:=5 ' 5 for
ppPasteOLEObject

' Add another slide for the table
Set pptSlide = pptPresentation.Slides.Add(2, 1) ' 1
for ppLayoutTitle

' Define the range to copy (assuming the table is in
range A1:C10)
Set tableRange =
excelWorkbook.Sheets("Sheet1").Range("A1:C10")

' Copy the table from Excel
tableRange.Copy

' Paste the table into the PowerPoint slide
pptSlide.Shapes.PasteSpecial DataType:=0 ' 0 for
ppPasteDefault

' Save the presentation
pptPresentation.SaveAs presentationPath

' Clean up
excelWorkbook.Close SaveChanges:=False
excelApp.Quit
Set tableRange = Nothing
Set excelChart = Nothing
Set excelWorkbook = Nothing
Set excelApp = Nothing
```

```
' Update linked data in the presentation
For Each pptSlide In pptPresentation.Slides
    For Each shape In pptSlide.Shapes
        If shape.Type = 12 Then ' 12 for
msoLinkedOLEObject
            shape.LinkFormat.Update
        End If
    Next shape
Next pptSlide
End Sub
```

In this comprehensive example:

- We embed a chart and a table from Excel into a PowerPoint presentation.
- We link the chart so it updates automatically when the data changes.
- We update all linked data in the presentation.

By mastering these techniques for integrating data from Excel into PowerPoint, you can create dynamic presentations that always reflect the latest data, making your presentations more powerful and up-to-date. Keep practicing, and soon you'll be an expert at integrating and automating data in PowerPoint!

12. Presentation management

Managing a PowerPoint presentation efficiently involves more than just creating and formatting slides. You can also customize slide shows, automate slide transitions, and add animations to enhance your presentation. In this chapter, we'll explore how to create custom slide shows and automate slide transitions and animations using VBA.

Creating custom slide shows

A custom slide show allows you to present a subset of slides from your main presentation in a specific order. This can be useful when you need to tailor your presentation for different audiences without creating multiple presentations.

Here's how to create a custom slide show using VBA:

```vba
Sub CreateCustomSlideShow()
    Dim pptApp As Object
    Dim pptPresentation As Object
    Dim slideShowSettings As Object
    Dim customShow As Object

    ' Path to the presentation file
    Dim presentationPath As String
    presentationPath = "C:\path\to\your\Presentation.pptx"

    ' Create a new instance of PowerPoint
    Set pptApp = CreateObject("PowerPoint.Application")
    pptApp.Visible = True

    ' Open the presentation
    Set pptPresentation =
pptApp.Presentations.Open(presentationPath)

    ' Define the slides for the custom show
    Dim slidesArray As Variant
    slidesArray = Array(1, 3, 5) ' Display slides 1, 3,
and 5 in the custom show

    ' Create a custom slide show
    Set slideShowSettings =
pptPresentation.SlideShowSettings
    Set customShow =
slideShowSettings.NamedSlideShows.Add("CustomShow1",
slidesArray)

    ' Set the custom slide show to run
    slideShowSettings.StartingSlide = 1
    slideShowSettings.EndingSlide =
pptPresentation.Slides.Count
    slideShowSettings.AdvanceMode = 2 ' 2 for
ppSlideShowUseSlideTimings
```

```
        slideShowSettings.NamedSlideShow = "CustomShow1"
        slideShowSettings.LoopUntilStopped = msoTrue
        slideShowSettings.Run
    End Sub
```

In this example:

- We open an existing PowerPoint presentation.
- We define an array of slide numbers to include in the custom slide show.
- We create the custom slide show and set it to run with specific settings.

Automating slide transitions and animations

Automating slide transitions

Slide transitions can be automated to enhance the flow of your presentation. Here's how to set up automatic slide transitions using VBA:

```
Sub AutomateSlideTransitions()
    Dim pptApp As Object
    Dim pptPresentation As Object
    Dim slide As Object

    ' Path to the presentation file
    Dim presentationPath As String
    presentationPath = "C:\path\to\your\Presentation.pptx"

    ' Create a new instance of PowerPoint
    Set pptApp = CreateObject("PowerPoint.Application")
    pptApp.Visible = True

    ' Open the presentation
    Set pptPresentation =
pptApp.Presentations.Open(presentationPath)

    ' Loop through each slide and set transition effects
    For Each slide In pptPresentation.Slides
        With slide.SlideShowTransition
```

```
                        .EntryEffect = 4 ' 4 for ppEffectFade
                        .AdvanceOnTime = msoTrue
                        .AdvanceTime = 3 ' Advance to the next slide
        after 3 seconds
                End With
        Next slide
    End Sub
```

In this example:

- We open an existing PowerPoint presentation.
- We loop through each slide and set a fade transition effect that advances to the next slide after 3 seconds.

Automating slide animations

Adding animations to slide objects can make your presentation more dynamic. Here's how to automate slide animations using VBA:

```
    Sub AutomateSlideAnimations()
        Dim pptApp As Object
        Dim pptPresentation As Object
        Dim slide As Object
        Dim shape As Object
        Dim animationSettings As Object

        ' Path to the presentation file
        Dim presentationPath As String
        presentationPath = "C:\path\to\your\Presentation.pptx"

        ' Create a new instance of PowerPoint
        Set pptApp = CreateObject("PowerPoint.Application")
        pptApp.Visible = True

        ' Open the presentation
        Set pptPresentation =
    pptApp.Presentations.Open(presentationPath)

        ' Loop through each slide and add animations to shapes
        For Each slide In pptPresentation.Slides
```

```
            For Each shape In slide.Shapes
                ' Add an entrance animation to the shape
                Set animationSettings =
    shape.AnimationSettings
                    animationSettings.EntryEffect = 1 ' 1 for
    ppEffectAppear
                    animationSettings.AdvanceMode = 1 ' 1 for
    ppAdvanceOnTime
                    animationSettings.AdvanceTime = 0.5 ' Start
    animation after 0.5 seconds
            Next shape
        Next slide
    End Sub
```

In this example:

- We open an existing PowerPoint presentation.
- We loop through each slide and each shape on the slide.
- We add an entrance animation that makes the shape appear after 0.5 seconds.

Putting it all together

Let's create a comprehensive example that combines custom slide shows, slide transitions, and animations.

```
    Sub ManagePresentation()
        Dim pptApp As Object
        Dim pptPresentation As Object
        Dim slideShowSettings As Object
        Dim customShow As Object
        Dim slide As Object
        Dim shape As Object
        Dim animationSettings As Object

        ' Path to the presentation file
        Dim presentationPath As String
        presentationPath = "C:\path\to\your\Presentation.pptx"

        ' Create a new instance of PowerPoint
```

```vba
    Set pptApp = CreateObject("PowerPoint.Application")
    pptApp.Visible = True

    ' Open the presentation
    Set pptPresentation =
pptApp.Presentations.Open(presentationPath)

    ' Define the slides for the custom show
    Dim slidesArray As Variant
    slidesArray = Array(1, 3, 5) ' Display slides 1, 3,
and 5 in the custom show

    ' Create a custom slide show
    Set slideShowSettings =
pptPresentation.SlideShowSettings
    Set customShow =
slideShowSettings.NamedSlideShows.Add("CustomShow1",
slidesArray)

    ' Set the custom slide show to run
    slideShowSettings.StartingSlide = 1
    slideShowSettings.EndingSlide =
pptPresentation.Slides.Count
    slideShowSettings.AdvanceMode = 2 ' 2 for
ppSlideShowUseSlideTimings
    slideShowSettings.NamedSlideShow = "CustomShow1"
    slideShowSettings.LoopUntilStopped = msoTrue

    ' Loop through each slide and set transition effects
    For Each slide In pptPresentation.Slides
        With slide.SlideShowTransition
            .EntryEffect = 4 ' 4 for ppEffectFade
            .AdvanceOnTime = msoTrue
            .AdvanceTime = 3 ' Advance to the next slide
after 3 seconds
        End With
```

```
        ' Add animations to shapes on each slide
        For Each shape In slide.Shapes
            ' Add an entrance animation to the shape
            Set animationSettings =
shape.AnimationSettings
            animationSettings.EntryEffect = 1 ' 1 for
ppEffectAppear
            animationSettings.AdvanceMode = 1 ' 1 for
ppAdvanceOnTime
            animationSettings.AdvanceTime = 0.5 ' Start
animation after 0.5 seconds
        Next shape
    Next slide

    ' Run the custom slide show
    slideShowSettings.Run
End Sub
```

In this comprehensive example:

- We create a custom slide show that includes specific slides.
- We set slide transitions for each slide.
- We add animations to shapes on each slide.
- We run the custom slide show with the specified settings.

By mastering these techniques for creating custom slide shows and automating slide transitions and animations, you can make your PowerPoint presentations more engaging and professional. Keep practicing, and soon you'll be able to manage complex presentations with ease!

Chapter 5: Automating Outlook tasks

13. Email automation

Automating email tasks can save you a lot of time, especially when you need to send the same type of email repeatedly or to a large list of recipients. In this chapter, we'll explore how to send emails directly from Excel using VBA and how to customize email templates for a personalized touch.

Sending emails from Excel

Setting up email automation

To send emails from Excel, you'll need to use VBA to interact with Outlook. Here's a basic example of how to send an email from Excel:

```
Sub SendEmail()
    Dim outlookApp As Object
    Dim outlookMail As Object
    Dim recipient As String
    Dim subject As String
    Dim body As String

    ' Create a new instance of Outlook
    Set outlookApp = CreateObject("Outlook.Application")
    Set outlookMail = outlookApp.CreateItem(0) ' 0 for
olMailItem

    ' Define email properties
    recipient = "recipient@example.com"
    subject = "Test Email"
    body = "Hello, this is a test email sent from Excel."

    ' Set up the email
    With outlookMail
```

```vba
        .To = recipient
        .Subject = subject
        .Body = body
        .Send
    End With

    ' Clean up
    Set outlookMail = Nothing
    Set outlookApp = Nothing
End Sub
```

In this example:

- We create a new instance of Outlook.
- We define the recipient, subject, and body of the email.
- We set up and send the email.

Sending emails to multiple recipients

If you have a list of recipients in an Excel worksheet, you can loop through the list to send personalized emails to each recipient.

```vba
Sub SendEmailsFromList()
    Dim outlookApp As Object
    Dim outlookMail As Object
    Dim ws As Worksheet
    Dim lastRow As Long
    Dim i As Long
    Dim recipient As String
    Dim subject As String
    Dim body As String

    ' Create a new instance of Outlook
    Set outlookApp = CreateObject("Outlook.Application")

    ' Define the worksheet and get the last row of data
    Set ws = ThisWorkbook.Sheets("Sheet1")
    lastRow = ws.Cells(ws.Rows.Count, "A").End(xlUp).Row

    ' Loop through the list of recipients
```

```
        For i = 2 To lastRow ' Assuming the first row is a
header
            recipient = ws.Cells(i, 1).Value
            subject = "Personalized Email"
            body = "Hello " & ws.Cells(i, 2).Value & "," &
vbCrLf & "This is a personalized email sent from Excel."

            ' Create and send the email
            Set outlookMail = outlookApp.CreateItem(0) ' 0 for
olMailItem
            With outlookMail
                .To = recipient
                .Subject = subject
                .Body = body
                .Send
            End With

            ' Clean up
            Set outlookMail = Nothing
        Next i

        ' Clean up
        Set outlookApp = Nothing
    End Sub
```

In this example:

- We loop through a list of recipients in an Excel worksheet.
- We personalize the subject and body of each email.
- We create and send the email for each recipient.

Customizing email templates

Creating an email template

You can create an email template in Outlook and use VBA to customize it before sending. Here's how to set up and use an email template:

Create a template in Outlook:

- Open Outlook and create a new email.
- Add the subject, body, and any formatting you want to include in your template.
- Save the email as a template: *File > Save As* and choose *Outlook Template (*.oft)*.

Using an email template with VBA

You can use VBA to open the template, customize it, and send the email. Here's an example:

```
Sub SendTemplateEmail()
    Dim outlookApp As Object
    Dim outlookMail As Object
    Dim templatePath As String
    Dim recipient As String

    ' Path to the email template
    templatePath = "C:\path\to\your\template.oft"

    ' Create a new instance of Outlook
    Set outlookApp = CreateObject("Outlook.Application")

    ' Open the email template
    Set outlookMail =
outlookApp.CreateItemFromTemplate(templatePath)

    ' Define the recipient and customize the email
    recipient = "recipient@example.com"

    With outlookMail
        .To = recipient
        .Subject = "Customized Email Subject"
        .HTMLBody = Replace(.HTMLBody, "Dear [Name],",
"Dear John,")
        .Send
    End With
```

```
                    ' Clean up
                    Set outlookMail = Nothing
                    Set outlookApp = Nothing
              End Sub
```

In this example:

- We open an existing email template.
- We customize the recipient, subject, and body of the email.
- We send the customized email.

Using placeholders in templates

To make your templates more flexible, you can use placeholders in the email body and replace them with actual values using VBA.

```
        Sub SendPersonalizedTemplateEmails()
              Dim outlookApp As Object
              Dim outlookMail As Object
              Dim templatePath As String
              Dim ws As Worksheet
              Dim lastRow As Long
              Dim i As Long
              Dim recipient As String
              Dim name As String
              Dim subject As String

              ' Path to the email template
              templatePath = "C:\path\to\your\template.oft"

              ' Create a new instance of Outlook
              Set outlookApp = CreateObject("Outlook.Application")

              ' Define the worksheet and get the last row of data
              Set ws = ThisWorkbook.Sheets("Sheet1")
              lastRow = ws.Cells(ws.Rows.Count, "A").End(xlUp).Row

              ' Loop through the list of recipients
              For i = 2 To lastRow ' Assuming the first row is a
        header
```

```
            recipient = ws.Cells(i, 1).Value
            name = ws.Cells(i, 2).Value
            subject = "Personalized Email"

            ' Open the email template
            Set outlookMail =
outlookApp.CreateItemFromTemplate(templatePath)

            ' Customize the email
            With outlookMail
                .To = recipient
                .Subject = subject
                .HTMLBody = Replace(.HTMLBody, "[Name]", name)
                .Send
            End With

            ' Clean up
            Set outlookMail = Nothing
        Next i

        ' Clean up
        Set outlookApp = Nothing
    End Sub
```

In this example:

- We loop through a list of recipients in an Excel worksheet.
- We open an email template for each recipient.
- We replace the placeholder [Name] with the actual name from the worksheet.
- We send the customized email for each recipient.

By mastering email automation and customizing email templates, you can efficiently manage your email communications directly from Excel. Keep practicing these techniques, and soon you'll be able to automate even the most complex email tasks with ease!

14. Calendar management

Managing your calendar efficiently can help you stay organized and ensure that you never miss important events or meetings. With VBA, you can automate the creation and management of calendar events and meeting requests in Outlook. In this chapter, we'll explore how to create and manage calendar events and automate meeting requests using VBA.

Creating and managing calendar events

Creating a calendar event

Let's start by creating a basic calendar event using VBA.

```
Sub CreateCalendarEvent()
    Dim outlookApp As Object
    Dim outlookEvent As Object

    ' Create a new instance of Outlook
    Set outlookApp = CreateObject("Outlook.Application")

    ' Create a new calendar event
    Set outlookEvent = outlookApp.CreateItem(1) ' 1 for
olAppointmentItem

    ' Set up the calendar event
    With outlookEvent
        .Subject = "Project Meeting"
        .Start = "2023-08-15 10:00 AM"
        .Duration = 60 ' Duration in minutes
        .Location = "Conference Room"
        .Body = "Discuss project milestones and
deadlines."
        .ReminderSet = True
        .ReminderMinutesBeforeStart = 15 ' Reminder 15
minutes before start
        .BusyStatus = 2 ' 2 for olBusy
        .Save
```

```
        End With

        ' Clean up
        Set outlookEvent = Nothing
        Set outlookApp = Nothing
    End Sub
```

In this example:

- We create a new instance of Outlook.
- We create a new calendar event and set properties like the subject, start time, duration, location, body, reminder, and busy status.

Updating an existing calendar event

You can also update existing calendar events by searching for them and modifying their properties.

```
    Sub UpdateCalendarEvent()
        Dim outlookApp As Object
        Dim outlookNamespace As Object
        Dim calendarFolder As Object
        Dim outlookEvent As Object
        Dim found As Boolean

        ' Create a new instance of Outlook
        Set outlookApp = CreateObject("Outlook.Application")
        Set outlookNamespace = outlookApp.GetNamespace("MAPI")
        Set calendarFolder =
    outlookNamespace.GetDefaultFolder(9) ' 9 for
    olFolderCalendar

        ' Search for the calendar event by subject
        found = False
        For Each outlookEvent In calendarFolder.Items
            If outlookEvent.Subject = "Project Meeting" Then
                found = True
                Exit For
            End If
        Next outlookEvent
```

```
        ' Update the calendar event if found
    If found Then
        With outlookEvent
            .Start = "2023-08-15 11:00 AM" ' Change start
time
            .Duration = 90 ' Change duration to 90 minutes
            .Location = "Main Conference Room" ' Change
location
            .Save
        End With
    Else
        MsgBox "Event not found."
    End If

    ' Clean up
    Set outlookEvent = Nothing
    Set calendarFolder = Nothing
    Set outlookNamespace = Nothing
    Set outlookApp = Nothing
End Sub
```

In this example:

- We search for an existing calendar event by its subject.
- If the event is found, we update its start time, duration, and location.

Automating meeting requests

Creating a meeting request

Meeting requests are similar to calendar events but include attendees. Here's how to create a meeting request using VBA:

```
Sub CreateMeetingRequest()
    Dim outlookApp As Object
    Dim outlookMeeting As Object

    ' Create a new instance of Outlook
    Set outlookApp = CreateObject("Outlook.Application")
```

```vba
        ' Create a new meeting request
        Set outlookMeeting = outlookApp.CreateItem(1) ' 1 for
    olAppointmentItem

        ' Set up the meeting request
        With outlookMeeting
            .Subject = "Team Meeting"
            .Start = "2023-08-20 2:00 PM"
            .Duration = 60 ' Duration in minutes
            .Location = "Meeting Room A"
            .Body = "Discuss team progress and next steps."
            .ReminderSet = True
            .ReminderMinutesBeforeStart = 30 ' Reminder 30
    minutes before start
            .BusyStatus = 2 ' 2 for olBusy

            ' Add required attendees
            .Recipients.Add "employee1@example.com"
            .Recipients.Add "employee2@example.com"

            ' Add optional attendees
            .Recipients.Add "manager@example.com"
            .Recipients(3).Type = 2 ' 2 for optional attendee

            .Send
        End With

        ' Clean up
        Set outlookMeeting = Nothing
        Set outlookApp = Nothing
    End Sub
```

In this example:

- We create a new meeting request and set properties like the subject, start time, duration, location, body, reminder, and busy status.

- We add required and optional attendees to the meeting request and send it.

Updating a meeting request

Updating a meeting request is similar to updating a calendar event. You can search for the meeting by its subject and modify its properties.

```vba
Sub UpdateMeetingRequest()
    Dim outlookApp As Object
    Dim outlookNamespace As Object
    Dim calendarFolder As Object
    Dim outlookMeeting As Object
    Dim found As Boolean

    ' Create a new instance of Outlook
    Set outlookApp = CreateObject("Outlook.Application")
    Set outlookNamespace = outlookApp.GetNamespace("MAPI")
    Set calendarFolder =
outlookNamespace.GetDefaultFolder(9) ' 9 for
olFolderCalendar

    ' Search for the meeting request by subject
    found = False
    For Each outlookMeeting In calendarFolder.Items
        If outlookMeeting.Subject = "Team Meeting" And
outlookMeeting.MeetingStatus = 1 Then ' 1 for olMeeting
            found = True
            Exit For
        End If
    Next outlookMeeting

    ' Update the meeting request if found
    If found Then
        With outlookMeeting
            .Start = "2023-08-20 3:00 PM" ' Change start
time
            .Duration = 90 ' Change duration to 90 minutes
```

```
                .Location = "Main Meeting Room" ' Change
        location
                .Recipients.Add "newmember@example.com" ' Add
        a new attendee
                .Save
                .Send ' Resend the updated meeting request
            End With
        Else
            MsgBox "Meeting not found."
        End If


        ' Clean up
        Set outlookMeeting = Nothing
        Set calendarFolder = Nothing
        Set outlookNamespace = Nothing
        Set outlookApp = Nothing
    End Sub
```

In this example:

- We search for an existing meeting request by its subject.
- If the meeting request is found, we update its start time, duration, location, and add a new attendee.

Putting it all together

Let's create a comprehensive example that demonstrates how to create and update calendar events and meeting requests using VBA.

```
        Sub ManageCalendarAndMeetings()
            Dim outlookApp As Object
            Dim outlookNamespace As Object
            Dim calendarFolder As Object
            Dim outlookEvent As Object
            Dim outlookMeeting As Object
            Dim found As Boolean

            ' Create a new instance of Outlook
            Set outlookApp = CreateObject("Outlook.Application")
            Set outlookNamespace = outlookApp.GetNamespace("MAPI")
```

```vba
    Set calendarFolder =
outlookNamespace.GetDefaultFolder(9) ' 9 for
olFolderCalendar

    ' Create a new calendar event
    Set outlookEvent = outlookApp.CreateItem(1) ' 1 for
olAppointmentItem
    With outlookEvent
        .Subject = "Project Kickoff"
        .Start = "2023-08-25 10:00 AM"
        .Duration = 120 ' Duration in minutes
        .Location = "Conference Room A"
        .Body = "Initial project meeting to discuss scope
and deliverables."
        .ReminderSet = True
        .ReminderMinutesBeforeStart = 20 ' Reminder 20
minutes before start
        .BusyStatus = 2 ' 2 for olBusy
        .Save
    End With

    ' Search for an existing meeting request
    found = False
    For Each outlookMeeting In calendarFolder.Items
        If outlookMeeting.Subject = "Team Meeting" And
outlookMeeting.MeetingStatus = 1 Then ' 1 for olMeeting
            found = True
            Exit For
        End If
    Next outlookMeeting

    ' Update the meeting request if found
    If found Then
        With outlookMeeting
            .Start = "2023-08-20 3:00 PM" ' Change start
time
```

```vba
                .Duration = 90 ' Change duration to 90 minutes
                .Location = "Main Meeting Room" ' Change
location
                .Recipients.Add "newmember@example.com" ' Add
a new attendee
                .Save
                .Send ' Resend the updated meeting request
            End With
        Else
            ' Create a new meeting request if not found
            Set outlookMeeting = outlookApp.CreateItem(1) ' 1
for olAppointmentItem
            With outlookMeeting
                .Subject = "Team Meeting"
                .Start = "2023-08-20 2:00 PM"
                .Duration = 60 ' Duration in minutes
                .Location = "Meeting Room A"
                .Body = "Discuss team progress and next
steps."
                .ReminderSet = True
                .ReminderMinutesBeforeStart = 30 ' Reminder 30
minutes before start
                .BusyStatus = 2 ' 2 for olBusy
                .Recipients.Add "employee1@example.com"
                .Recipients.Add "employee2@example.com"
                .Recipients.Add "manager@example.com"
                .Recipients(3).Type = 2 ' 2 for optional
attendee
                .Send
            End With
        End If

        ' Clean up
        Set outlookEvent = Nothing
        Set outlookMeeting = Nothing
        Set calendarFolder = Nothing
```

```
            Set outlookNamespace = Nothing
            Set outlookApp = Nothing
        End Sub
```

In this comprehensive example:

- We create a new calendar event for a project kickoff meeting.
- We search for an existing team meeting request. If found, we update its properties and add a new attendee. If not found, we create a new meeting request.

By mastering these techniques for creating and managing calendar events and automating meeting requests, you can efficiently handle your Outlook calendar directly from Excel. Keep practicing, and soon you'll be able to automate all your calendar management tasks with ease!

15. Task management

Keeping track of tasks can be a hassle, but with VBA, you can automate the creation and tracking of tasks in Outlook. This chapter will show you how to create and manage tasks automatically and integrate tasks with other Office applications for a more streamlined workflow.

Automating task creation and tracking

Creating a Task

Let's start by creating a simple task in Outlook using VBA:

```
        Sub CreateTask()
            Dim outlookApp As Object
            Dim outlookTask As Object

            ' Create a new instance of Outlook
            Set outlookApp = CreateObject("Outlook.Application")

            ' Create a new task
            Set outlookTask = outlookApp.CreateItem(3) ' 3 for
        olTaskItem

            ' Set up the task
            With outlookTask
```

```
            .Subject = "Complete Project Report"
            .DueDate = "2023-08-30"
            .Body = "Remember to include the latest financials
    and team feedback."
            .ReminderSet = True
            .ReminderTime = "2023-08-29 10:00 AM"
            .Importance = 2 ' 2 for high importance
            .Save
        End With

        ' Clean up
        Set outlookTask = Nothing
        Set outlookApp = Nothing
    End Sub
```

In this example:

- We create a new instance of Outlook.
- We create a new task and set properties like the subject, due date, body, reminder, and importance.

Tracking task progress

You can also automate the tracking of task progress. Here's how to update a task's status and progress:

```
    Sub UpdateTaskProgress()
        Dim outlookApp As Object
        Dim outlookNamespace As Object
        Dim tasksFolder As Object
        Dim outlookTask As Object
        Dim found As Boolean

        ' Create a new instance of Outlook
        Set outlookApp = CreateObject("Outlook.Application")
        Set outlookNamespace = outlookApp.GetNamespace("MAPI")
        Set tasksFolder =
    outlookNamespace.GetDefaultFolder(13) ' 13 for
    olFolderTasks
```

```vba
        ' Search for the task by subject
        found = False
        For Each outlookTask In tasksFolder.Items
            If outlookTask.Subject = "Complete Project Report"
Then
                found = True
                Exit For
            End If
        Next outlookTask

        ' Update the task if found
        If found Then
            With outlookTask
                .Status = 1 ' 1 for olTaskInProgress
                .PercentComplete = 50 ' 50% complete
                .Save
            End With
        Else
            MsgBox "Task not found."
        End If

        ' Clean up
        Set outlookTask = Nothing
        Set tasksFolder = Nothing
        Set outlookNamespace = Nothing
        Set outlookApp = Nothing
    End Sub
```

In this example:

- We search for an existing task by its subject.
- If the task is found, we update its status and percent complete properties.

Integrating tasks with other Office applications

Creating tasks from Excel data

You can create tasks from a list of tasks in an Excel worksheet. Here's how:

```vba
Sub CreateTasksFromExcel()
    Dim outlookApp As Object
    Dim outlookTask As Object
    Dim ws As Worksheet
    Dim lastRow As Long
    Dim i As Long
    Dim subject As String
    Dim dueDate As String
    Dim body As String

    ' Create a new instance of Outlook
    Set outlookApp = CreateObject("Outlook.Application")

    ' Define the worksheet and get the last row of data
    Set ws = ThisWorkbook.Sheets("Tasks")
    lastRow = ws.Cells(ws.Rows.Count, "A").End(xlUp).Row

    ' Loop through the list of tasks in Excel
    For i = 2 To lastRow ' Assuming the first row is a
header
        subject = ws.Cells(i, 1).Value
        dueDate = ws.Cells(i, 2).Value
        body = ws.Cells(i, 3).Value

        ' Create and set up the task
        Set outlookTask = outlookApp.CreateItem(3) ' 3 for
olTaskItem
        With outlookTask
            .Subject = subject
            .DueDate = dueDate
            .Body = body
            .ReminderSet = True
            .ReminderTime = DateAdd("d", -1, dueDate) & "
9:00 AM"
            .Save
        End With
```

```
        ' Clean up
        Set outlookTask = Nothing
    Next i

        ' Clean up
        Set outlookApp = Nothing
    End Sub
```

In this example:

- We loop through a list of tasks in an Excel worksheet.
- For each task, we create a new Outlook task and set its properties based on the Excel data.

Linking tasks to emails

Sometimes, it's helpful to link tasks to specific emails. Here's how to create a task with a link to an email:

```
Sub CreateTaskWithEmailLink()
    Dim outlookApp As Object
    Dim outlookMail As Object
    Dim outlookTask As Object
    Dim mailLink As String

    ' Create a new instance of Outlook
    Set outlookApp = CreateObject("Outlook.Application")

    ' Create a new task
    Set outlookTask = outlookApp.CreateItem(3) ' 3 for
olTaskItem

    ' Get the selected email
    Set outlookMail =
outlookApp.ActiveExplorer.Selection.Item(1)

    ' Create a link to the email
    mailLink = "Outlook:" & outlookMail.EntryID
```

```vba
    ' Set up the task
    With outlookTask
        .Subject = "Follow up on email"
        .DueDate = Date + 2
        .Body = "Please follow up on the attached email: "
& vbCrLf & mailLink
        .ReminderSet = True
        .ReminderTime = Date + 1 & " 10:00 AM"
        .Save
    End With

    ' Clean up
    Set outlookTask = Nothing
    Set outlookMail = Nothing
    Set outlookApp = Nothing
End Sub
```

In this example:

- We create a new task and link it to a selected email in Outlook.
- The task body includes a link to the email for easy reference.

Putting it all together

Let's create a comprehensive example that demonstrates how to create and manage tasks from Excel and link them to emails.

```vba
Sub ManageTasks()
    Dim outlookApp As Object
    Dim outlookNamespace As Object
    Dim tasksFolder As Object
    Dim outlookTask As Object
    Dim ws As Worksheet
    Dim lastRow As Long
    Dim i As Long
    Dim subject As String
    Dim dueDate As String
    Dim body As String

    ' Create a new instance of Outlook
```

```
        Set outlookApp = CreateObject("Outlook.Application")
        Set outlookNamespace = outlookApp.GetNamespace("MAPI")
        Set tasksFolder =
outlookNamespace.GetDefaultFolder(13) ' 13 for
olFolderTasks

        ' Define the worksheet and get the last row of data
        Set ws = ThisWorkbook.Sheets("Tasks")
        lastRow = ws.Cells(ws.Rows.Count, "A").End(xlUp).Row

        ' Loop through the list of tasks in Excel
        For i = 2 To lastRow ' Assuming the first row is a
header
            subject = ws.Cells(i, 1).Value
            dueDate = ws.Cells(i, 2).Value
            body = ws.Cells(i, 3).Value

            ' Create and set up the task
            Set outlookTask = outlookApp.CreateItem(3) ' 3 for
olTaskItem
            With outlookTask
                .Subject = subject
                .DueDate = dueDate
                .Body = body
                .ReminderSet = True
                .ReminderTime = DateAdd("d", -1, dueDate) & "
9:00 AM"
                .Save
            End With

            ' Clean up
            Set outlookTask = Nothing
        Next i

        ' Search for an existing task by subject
        Dim found As Boolean
```

```vba
        found = False
        For Each outlookTask In tasksFolder.Items
            If outlookTask.Subject = "Complete Project Report"
    Then
                found = True
                Exit For
            End If
        Next outlookTask

        ' Update the task if found
        If found Then
            With outlookTask
                .Status = 1 ' 1 for olTaskInProgress
                .PercentComplete = 50 ' 50% complete
                .Save
            End With
        Else
            MsgBox "Task not found."
        End If

        ' Clean up
        Set outlookTask = Nothing
        Set tasksFolder = Nothing
        Set outlookNamespace = Nothing
        Set outlookApp = Nothing
    End Sub
```

In this comprehensive example:

- We create tasks from a list in Excel.
- We search for an existing task and update its progress if found.

By mastering these techniques for automating task creation and tracking, and integrating tasks with other Office applications, you can efficiently manage your tasks directly from Excel. Keep practicing, and soon you'll be able to automate all your task management tasks with ease!

Chapter 6: Cross-application automation

16. Integrating Excel with Word and PowerPoint

In the business world, it's common to create reports and presentations that combine data from multiple sources. Automating these processes can save you a lot of time and ensure consistency across your documents and presentations. In this chapter, we'll explore how to integrate Excel with Word and PowerPoint to create reports and automate updates.

Creating reports combining data from multiple sources

Combining data from Excel into a Word report

Let's start by combining data from an Excel spreadsheet into a Word document to create a report.

```
Sub CreateWordReportFromExcel()
    Dim excelApp As Object
    Dim excelWorkbook As Object
    Dim dataRange As Range
    Dim wordApp As Object
    Dim wordDoc As Object
    Dim wordTable As Object

    ' Paths to the files
    Dim excelFilePath As String
    Dim wordFilePath As String
    excelFilePath = "C:\path\to\your\ExcelFile.xlsx"
    wordFilePath = "C:\path\to\your\WordReport.docx"

    ' Create a new instance of Excel and open the workbook
    Set excelApp = CreateObject("Excel.Application")
```

```vba
        Set excelWorkbook =
    excelApp.Workbooks.Open(excelFilePath)

        ' Define the range of data to copy
        Set dataRange =
    excelWorkbook.Sheets("Sheet1").Range("A1:C10")

        ' Copy the data
        dataRange.Copy

        ' Create a new instance of Word and open the document
        Set wordApp = CreateObject("Word.Application")
        wordApp.Visible = True
        Set wordDoc = wordApp.Documents.Add

        ' Paste the data as a table in Word
        wordDoc.Content.PasteExcelTable LinkedToExcel:=False,
    WordFormatting:=True, RTF:=False

        ' Save the Word document
        wordDoc.SaveAs2 wordFilePath

        ' Clean up
        excelWorkbook.Close SaveChanges:=False
        excelApp.Quit
        Set dataRange = Nothing
        Set excelWorkbook = Nothing
        Set excelApp = Nothing
        Set wordTable = Nothing
        Set wordDoc = Nothing
        Set wordApp = Nothing
    End Sub
```

In this example:

- We open an Excel workbook and copy a range of data.
- We create a new Word document and paste the copied data as a table.

- We save the Word document.

Combining data from Excel into a PowerPoint presentation

Next, let's combine data from an Excel spreadsheet into a PowerPoint presentation to create a dynamic report.

```
Sub CreatePowerPointFromExcel()
    Dim excelApp As Object
    Dim excelWorkbook As Object
    Dim dataRange As Range
    Dim pptApp As Object
    Dim pptPresentation As Object
    Dim pptSlide As Object
    Dim pptTable As Object

    ' Paths to the files
    Dim excelFilePath As String
    Dim pptFilePath As String
    excelFilePath = "C:\path\to\your\ExcelFile.xlsx"
    pptFilePath =
"C:\path\to\your\PowerPointPresentation.pptx"

    ' Create a new instance of Excel and open the workbook
    Set excelApp = CreateObject("Excel.Application")
    Set excelWorkbook =
excelApp.Workbooks.Open(excelFilePath)

    ' Define the range of data to copy
    Set dataRange =
excelWorkbook.Sheets("Sheet1").Range("A1:C10")

    ' Copy the data
    dataRange.Copy

    ' Create a new instance of PowerPoint and add a
presentation
    Set pptApp = CreateObject("PowerPoint.Application")
```

```
        pptApp.Visible = True
        Set pptPresentation = pptApp.Presentations.Add

        ' Add a new slide
        Set pptSlide = pptPresentation.Slides.Add(1, 1) ' 1
    for ppLayoutTitle

        ' Paste the data as a table in PowerPoint
        pptSlide.Shapes.PasteSpecial DataType:=0 ' 0 for
    ppPasteDefault

        ' Save the PowerPoint presentation
        pptPresentation.SaveAs pptFilePath

        ' Clean up
        excelWorkbook.Close SaveChanges:=False
        excelApp.Quit
        Set dataRange = Nothing
        Set excelWorkbook = Nothing
        Set excelApp = Nothing
        Set pptSlide = Nothing
        Set pptTable = Nothing
        Set pptPresentation = Nothing
        Set pptApp = Nothing
    End Sub
```

In this example:

- We open an Excel workbook and copy a range of data.
- We create a new PowerPoint presentation and add a slide.
- We paste the copied data as a table into the slide.
- We save the PowerPoint presentation.

Automating document and presentation updates

Updating a Word document from Excel

You can update an existing Word document with new data from Excel. Here's how:

```vba
Sub UpdateWordDocumentFromExcel()
    Dim excelApp As Object
    Dim excelWorkbook As Object
    Dim dataRange As Range
    Dim wordApp As Object
    Dim wordDoc As Object
    Dim wordTable As Object

    ' Paths to the files
    Dim excelFilePath As String
    Dim wordFilePath As String
    excelFilePath = "C:\path\to\your\ExcelFile.xlsx"
    wordFilePath = "C:\path\to\your\WordReport.docx"

    ' Create a new instance of Excel and open the workbook
    Set excelApp = CreateObject("Excel.Application")
    Set excelWorkbook =
excelApp.Workbooks.Open(excelFilePath)

    ' Define the range of data to copy
    Set dataRange =
excelWorkbook.Sheets("Sheet1").Range("A1:C10")

    ' Copy the data
    dataRange.Copy

    ' Create a new instance of Word and open the document
    Set wordApp = CreateObject("Word.Application")
    wordApp.Visible = True
    Set wordDoc = wordApp.Documents.Open(wordFilePath)

    ' Find the table to update (assuming the table is the
first one)
    Set wordTable = wordDoc.Tables(1)

    ' Delete the existing content and paste the new data
```

```
        wordTable.Range.Delete
        wordTable.Range.PasteExcelTable LinkedToExcel:=False,
WordFormatting:=True, RTF:=False

        ' Save and close the Word document
        wordDoc.Save
        wordDoc.Close

        ' Clean up
        excelWorkbook.Close SaveChanges:=False
        excelApp.Quit
        Set dataRange = Nothing
        Set excelWorkbook = Nothing
        Set excelApp = Nothing
        Set wordTable = Nothing
        Set wordDoc = Nothing
        Set wordApp = Nothing
    End Sub
```

In this example:

- We open an existing Word document.
- We find the first table in the document and update it with new data from Excel.
- We save and close the Word document.

Updating a PowerPoint presentation from Excel

You can also update an existing PowerPoint presentation with new data from Excel.

```
    Sub UpdatePowerPointFromExcel()
        Dim excelApp As Object
        Dim excelWorkbook As Object
        Dim dataRange As Range
        Dim pptApp As Object
        Dim pptPresentation As Object
        Dim pptSlide As Object
        Dim pptTable As Object
```

```vba
' Paths to the files
Dim excelFilePath As String
Dim pptFilePath As String
excelFilePath = "C:\path\to\your\ExcelFile.xlsx"
pptFilePath =
"C:\path\to\your\PowerPointPresentation.pptx"

' Create a new instance of Excel and open the workbook
Set excelApp = CreateObject("Excel.Application")
Set excelWorkbook =
excelApp.Workbooks.Open(excelFilePath)

' Define the range of data to copy
Set dataRange =
excelWorkbook.Sheets("Sheet1").Range("A1:C10")

' Copy the data
dataRange.Copy

' Create a new instance of PowerPoint and open the
presentation
Set pptApp = CreateObject("PowerPoint.Application")
pptApp.Visible = True
Set pptPresentation =
pptApp.Presentations.Open(pptFilePath)

' Find the slide to update (assuming the table is on
the first slide)
Set pptSlide = pptPresentation.Slides(1)

' Delete the existing table and paste the new data
pptSlide.Shapes(1).Delete
pptSlide.Shapes.PasteSpecial DataType:=0 ' 0 for
ppPasteDefault

' Save and close the PowerPoint presentation
```

```
            pptPresentation.Save
            pptPresentation.Close

            ' Clean up
            excelWorkbook.Close SaveChanges:=False
            excelApp.Quit
            Set dataRange = Nothing
            Set excelWorkbook = Nothing
            Set excelApp = Nothing
            Set pptSlide = Nothing
            Set pptTable = Nothing
            Set pptPresentation = Nothing
            Set pptApp = Nothing
        End Sub
```

In this example:

- We open an existing PowerPoint presentation.
- We find the first slide and update its content with new data from Excel.
- We save and close the PowerPoint presentation.

Putting it all together

Let's create a comprehensive example that demonstrates how to combine data from Excel into both Word and PowerPoint and automate updates.

```
        Sub UpdateDocumentsFromExcel()
            Dim excelApp As Object
            Dim excelWorkbook As Object
            Dim dataRange As Range
            Dim wordApp As Object
            Dim wordDoc As Object
            Dim wordTable As Object
            Dim pptApp As Object
            Dim pptPresentation As Object
            Dim pptSlide As Object

            ' Paths to the files
            Dim excelFilePath As String
```

```vba
        Dim wordFilePath As String
        Dim pptFilePath As String
        excelFilePath = "C:\path\to\your\ExcelFile.xlsx"
        wordFilePath = "C:\path\to\your\WordReport.docx"
        pptFilePath =
"C:\path\to\your\PowerPointPresentation.pptx"

        ' Create a new instance of Excel and open the workbook
        Set excelApp = CreateObject("Excel.Application")
        Set excelWorkbook =
excelApp.Workbooks.Open(excelFilePath)

        ' Define the range of data to copy
        Set dataRange =
excelWorkbook.Sheets("Sheet1").Range("A1:C10")

        ' Copy the data
        dataRange.Copy

        ' Update the Word document
        Set wordApp = CreateObject("Word.Application")
        wordApp.Visible = True
        Set wordDoc = wordApp.Documents.Open(wordFilePath)
        Set wordTable = wordDoc.Tables(1)
        wordTable.Range.Delete
        wordTable.Range.PasteExcelTable LinkedToExcel:=False,
WordFormatting:=True, RTF:=False
        wordDoc.Save
        wordDoc.Close

        ' Update the PowerPoint presentation
        Set pptApp = CreateObject("PowerPoint.Application")
        pptApp.Visible = True
        Set pptPresentation =
pptApp.Presentations.Open(pptFilePath)
        Set pptSlide = pptPresentation.Slides(1)
```

```
        pptSlide.Shapes(1).Delete
        pptSlide.Shapes.PasteSpecial DataType:=0 ' 0 for
    ppPasteDefault
        pptPresentation.Save
        pptPresentation.Close

        ' Clean up
        excelWorkbook.Close SaveChanges:=False
        excelApp.Quit
        Set dataRange = Nothing
        Set excelWorkbook = Nothing
        Set excelApp = Nothing
        Set wordTable = Nothing
        Set wordDoc = Nothing
        Set wordApp = Nothing
        Set pptSlide = Nothing
        Set pptPresentation = Nothing
        Set pptApp = Nothing
    End Sub
```

In this comprehensive example:

- We update an existing Word document and a PowerPoint presentation with new data from Excel.
- We ensure that the documents reflect the latest data by automating the process.

By mastering these techniques for integrating Excel with Word and PowerPoint, you can create dynamic reports and presentations that always reflect the most current data. Keep practicing, and soon you'll be able to automate complex cross-application tasks with ease!

17. Data exchange between applications

Transferring data between Excel, Word, and PowerPoint can be time-consuming if done manually. Fortunately, you can use VBA to automate this process, ensuring that your documents and presentations are always up-to-date. In this chapter, we'll explore how to transfer data between these applications and automate data synchronization.

Using VBA to transfer data between Excel, Word, and PowerPoint

Transferring data from Excel to Word

Let's start by transferring data from an Excel spreadsheet to a Word document. This can be useful for creating reports that require regular updates.

```vba
Sub TransferDataFromExcelToWord()
    Dim excelApp As Object
    Dim excelWorkbook As Object
    Dim dataRange As Range
    Dim wordApp As Object
    Dim wordDoc As Object

    ' Paths to the files
    Dim excelFilePath As String
    Dim wordFilePath As String
    excelFilePath = "C:\path\to\your\ExcelFile.xlsx"
    wordFilePath = "C:\path\to\your\WordReport.docx"

    ' Create a new instance of Excel and open the workbook
    Set excelApp = CreateObject("Excel.Application")
    Set excelWorkbook =
excelApp.Workbooks.Open(excelFilePath)

    ' Define the range of data to copy
    Set dataRange =
excelWorkbook.Sheets("Sheet1").Range("A1:C10")

    ' Copy the data
    dataRange.Copy

    ' Create a new instance of Word and open the document
    Set wordApp = CreateObject("Word.Application")
    wordApp.Visible = True
    Set wordDoc = wordApp.Documents.Open(wordFilePath)
```

```
      ' Paste the data as a table in Word
      wordDoc.Content.PasteExcelTable LinkedToExcel:=False,
  WordFormatting:=True, RTF:=False

      ' Save and close the Word document
      wordDoc.Save
      wordDoc.Close

      ' Clean up
      excelWorkbook.Close SaveChanges:=False
      excelApp.Quit
      Set dataRange = Nothing
      Set excelWorkbook = Nothing
      Set excelApp = Nothing
      Set wordDoc = Nothing
      Set wordApp = Nothing
  End Sub
```

In this example:

- We open an Excel workbook and copy a range of data.
- We create a new Word document and paste the copied data as a table.
- We save and close the Word document.

Transferring data from Excel to PowerPoint

Next, let's transfer data from an Excel spreadsheet to a PowerPoint presentation.

```
      Sub TransferDataFromExcelToPowerPoint()
          Dim excelApp As Object
          Dim excelWorkbook As Object
          Dim dataRange As Range
          Dim pptApp As Object
          Dim pptPresentation As Object
          Dim pptSlide As Object

          ' Paths to the files
```

```vba
    Dim excelFilePath As String
    Dim pptFilePath As String
    excelFilePath = "C:\path\to\your\ExcelFile.xlsx"
    pptFilePath =
"C:\path\to\your\PowerPointPresentation.pptx"

    ' Create a new instance of Excel and open the workbook
    Set excelApp = CreateObject("Excel.Application")
    Set excelWorkbook =
excelApp.Workbooks.Open(excelFilePath)

    ' Define the range of data to copy
    Set dataRange =
excelWorkbook.Sheets("Sheet1").Range("A1:C10")

    ' Copy the data
    dataRange.Copy

    ' Create a new instance of PowerPoint and add a
presentation
    Set pptApp = CreateObject("PowerPoint.Application")
    pptApp.Visible = True
    Set pptPresentation = pptApp.Presentations.Add

    ' Add a new slide
    Set pptSlide = pptPresentation.Slides.Add(1, 1) ' 1
for ppLayoutTitle

    ' Paste the data as a table in PowerPoint
    pptSlide.Shapes.PasteSpecial DataType:=0 ' 0 for
ppPasteDefault

    ' Save and close the PowerPoint presentation
    pptPresentation.SaveAs pptFilePath
    pptPresentation.Close
```

```
        ' Clean up
        excelWorkbook.Close SaveChanges:=False
        excelApp.Quit
        Set dataRange = Nothing
        Set excelWorkbook = Nothing
        Set excelApp = Nothing
        Set pptSlide = Nothing
        Set pptPresentation = Nothing
        Set pptApp = Nothing
    End Sub
```

In this example:

- We open an Excel workbook and copy a range of data.
- We create a new PowerPoint presentation and add a slide.
- We paste the copied data as a table into the slide.
- We save and close the PowerPoint presentation.

Automating data synchronization

Synchronizing data between Excel and Word

You can automate the synchronization of data between Excel and Word to ensure that your reports always reflect the latest information.

```
Sub SyncDataBetweenExcelAndWord()
    Dim excelApp As Object
    Dim excelWorkbook As Object
    Dim dataRange As Range
    Dim wordApp As Object
    Dim wordDoc As Object
    Dim wordTable As Object

    ' Paths to the files
    Dim excelFilePath As String
    Dim wordFilePath As String
    excelFilePath = "C:\path\to\your\ExcelFile.xlsx"
    wordFilePath = "C:\path\to\your\WordReport.docx"

    ' Create a new instance of Excel and open the workbook
```

```vba
    Set excelApp = CreateObject("Excel.Application")
    Set excelWorkbook = excelApp.Workbooks.Open(excelFilePath)

    ' Define the range of data to copy
    Set dataRange = excelWorkbook.Sheets("Sheet1").Range("A1:C10")

    ' Copy the data
    dataRange.Copy

    ' Create a new instance of Word and open the document
    Set wordApp = CreateObject("Word.Application")
    wordApp.Visible = True
    Set wordDoc = wordApp.Documents.Open(wordFilePath)

    ' Find the table to update (assuming the table is the first
one)
    Set wordTable = wordDoc.Tables(1)

    ' Delete the existing content and paste the new data
    wordTable.Range.Delete
    wordTable.Range.PasteExcelTable LinkedToExcel:=False,
WordFormatting:=True, RTF:=False

    ' Save and close the Word document
    wordDoc.Save
    wordDoc.Close

    ' Clean up
    excelWorkbook.Close SaveChanges:=False
    excelApp.Quit
    Set dataRange = Nothing
    Set excelWorkbook = Nothing
    Set excelApp = Nothing
    Set wordTable = Nothing
    Set wordDoc = Nothing
    Set wordApp = Nothing
```

```
End Sub
```

In this example:

- We open an Excel workbook and copy a range of data.
- We open an existing Word document and update its table with new data from Excel.
- We save and close the Word document.

Synchronizing data between Excel and PowerPoint

Similarly, you can automate the synchronization of data between Excel and PowerPoint.

```
Sub SyncDataBetweenExcelAndPowerPoint()
    Dim excelApp As Object
    Dim excelWorkbook As Object
    Dim dataRange As Range
    Dim pptApp As Object
    Dim pptPresentation As Object
    Dim pptSlide As Object

    ' Paths to the files
    Dim excelFilePath As String
    Dim pptFilePath As String
    excelFilePath = "C:\path\to\your\ExcelFile.xlsx"
    pptFilePath =
"C:\path\to\your\PowerPointPresentation.pptx"

    ' Create a new instance of Excel and open the workbook
    Set excelApp = CreateObject("Excel.Application")
    Set excelWorkbook =
excelApp.Workbooks.Open(excelFilePath)

    ' Define the range of data to copy
    Set dataRange =
excelWorkbook.Sheets("Sheet1").Range("A1:C10")

    ' Copy the data
    dataRange.Copy
```

```
        ' Create a new instance of PowerPoint and open the
    presentation
        Set pptApp = CreateObject("PowerPoint.Application")
        pptApp.Visible = True
        Set pptPresentation =
    pptApp.Presentations.Open(pptFilePath)

        ' Find the slide to update (assuming the table is on
    the first slide)
        Set pptSlide = pptPresentation.Slides(1)

        ' Delete the existing table and paste the new data
        pptSlide.Shapes(1).Delete
        pptSlide.Shapes.PasteSpecial DataType:=0 ' 0 for
    ppPasteDefault

        ' Save and close the PowerPoint presentation
        pptPresentation.Save
        pptPresentation.Close

        ' Clean up
        excelWorkbook.Close SaveChanges:=False
        excelApp.Quit
        Set dataRange = Nothing
        Set excelWorkbook = Nothing
        Set excelApp = Nothing
        Set pptSlide = Nothing
        Set pptPresentation = Nothing
        Set pptApp = Nothing
    End Sub
```

In this example:

- We open an Excel workbook and copy a range of data.
- We open an existing PowerPoint presentation and update its slide with new data from Excel.
- We save and close the PowerPoint presentation.

Putting it all together

Let's create a comprehensive example that demonstrates how to automate data transfer and synchronization between Excel, Word, and PowerPoint.

```
Sub SyncDataBetweenAllApplications()
    Dim excelApp As Object
    Dim excelWorkbook As Object
    Dim dataRange As Range
    Dim wordApp As Object
    Dim wordDoc As Object
    Dim wordTable As Object
    Dim pptApp As Object
    Dim pptPresentation As Object
    Dim pptSlide As Object

    ' Paths to the files
    Dim excelFilePath As String
    Dim wordFilePath As String
    Dim pptFilePath As String
    excelFilePath = "C:\path\to\your\ExcelFile.xlsx"
    wordFilePath = "C:\path\to\your\WordReport.docx"
    pptFilePath =
"C:\path\to\your\PowerPointPresentation.pptx"

    ' Create a new instance of Excel and open the workbook
    Set excelApp = CreateObject("Excel.Application")
    Set excelWorkbook =
excelApp.Workbooks.Open(excelFilePath)

    ' Define the range of data to copy
    Set dataRange =
excelWorkbook.Sheets("Sheet1").Range("A1:C10")

    ' Copy the data
    dataRange.Copy
```

```vba
    ' Update the Word document
    Set wordApp = CreateObject("Word.Application")
    wordApp.Visible = True
    Set wordDoc = wordApp.Documents.Open(wordFilePath)
    Set wordTable = wordDoc.Tables(1)
    wordTable.Range.Delete
    wordTable.Range.PasteExcelTable LinkedToExcel:=False,
WordFormatting:=True, RTF:=False
    wordDoc.Save
    wordDoc.Close

    ' Update the PowerPoint presentation
    Set pptApp = CreateObject("PowerPoint.Application")
    pptApp.Visible = True
    Set pptPresentation =
pptApp.Presentations.Open(pptFilePath)
    Set pptSlide = pptPresentation.Slides(1)
    pptSlide.Shapes(1).Delete
    pptSlide.Shapes.PasteSpecial DataType:=0 ' 0 for
ppPasteDefault
    pptPresentation.Save
    pptPresentation.Close

    ' Clean up
    excelWorkbook.Close SaveChanges:=False
    excelApp.Quit
    Set dataRange = Nothing
    Set excelWorkbook = Nothing
    Set excelApp = Nothing
    Set wordTable = Nothing
    Set wordDoc = Nothing
    Set wordApp = Nothing
    Set pptSlide = Nothing
    Set pptPresentation = Nothing
    Set pptApp = Nothing
End Sub
```

In this comprehensive example:

- We update an existing Word document and a PowerPoint presentation with new data from Excel.
- We ensure that the documents reflect the latest data by automating the process.

By mastering these techniques for transferring data between Excel, Word, and PowerPoint, and automating data synchronization, you can create dynamic and up-to-date reports and presentations. Keep practicing, and soon you'll be able to automate complex cross-application tasks with ease!

Chapter 7: Advanced VBA techniques

18. Error handling and debugging

When writing VBA code, it's essential to ensure that your macros can handle errors gracefully and that you can debug them efficiently. This chapter will cover how to implement robust error handling and provide techniques for debugging complex macros, making your VBA projects more reliable and easier to maintain.

Implementing robust error handling

Why error handling is important

Errors can occur for various reasons: invalid inputs, missing files, or unexpected conditions. Without proper error handling, your macro might crash, leading to data loss or other issues. Robust error handling helps you manage these situations gracefully and keeps your macros running smoothly.

Basic error handling with *On Error*

The simplest way to handle errors in VBA is using the On Error statement. Here's an example:

```
Sub BasicErrorHandling()
    On Error GoTo ErrorHandler

    ' Attempt to divide by zero (this will cause an error)
    Dim x As Integer
    x = 1 / 0

    MsgBox "This message won't be displayed due to the
error above."

    Exit Sub
```

```
ErrorHandler:
    MsgBox "An error occurred: " & Err.Description
End Sub
```

In this example:

- The *On Error GoTo ErrorHandler* statement tells VBA to jump to the *ErrorHandler* label if an error occurs.
- If an error occurs, a message box displays the error description.

Using *Resume* for error recovery

Sometimes, after handling an error, you might want to retry the operation or skip over it. The *Resume* statement helps you do this:

```
Sub ErrorRecovery()
    On Error GoTo ErrorHandler

    Dim x As Integer
    x = 1 / 0 ' This will cause an error

    MsgBox "This message won't be displayed due to the
error above."

    Exit Sub

ErrorHandler:
    MsgBox "An error occurred: " & Err.Description
    Resume Next ' Resume execution with the next statement
after the error
End Sub
```

In this example:

- After displaying the error message, the *Resume Next* statement allows the macro to continue with the next statement after the error.

Logging errors

For more complex macros, logging errors to a file can be very useful for debugging and monitoring purposes:

```
Sub LogErrors()
```

```
        On Error GoTo ErrorHandler

        Dim x As Integer
        x = 1 / 0 ' This will cause an error

        MsgBox "This message won't be displayed due to the
    error above."

        Exit Sub

    ErrorHandler:
        LogError "Error: " & Err.Description
        Resume Next
    End Sub

    Sub LogError(errorMessage As String)
        Dim logFile As String
        logFile = "C:\path\to\your\error_log.txt"

        Dim fileNum As Integer
        fileNum = FreeFile

        Open logFile For Append As #fileNum
        Print #fileNum, Now & " - " & errorMessage
        Close #fileNum
    End Sub
```

In this example:

- The *LogError* subroutine writes error messages to a text file, along with a timestamp.

Techniques for debugging complex macros

Using the VBA Debugger

The VBA debugger is a powerful tool that lets you step through your code, inspect variables, and evaluate expressions. Here are some key features:

- **Breakpoints:** Set breakpoints by clicking in the left margin next to a line of code. Execution will pause when it reaches a breakpoint, allowing you to inspect the state of your program.
- **Step Into (F8):** Executes your code one line at a time. This is useful for closely examining the behavior of your macro.
- **Step Over (Shift+F8):** Executes the next line of code but skips over any calls to other procedures. This is useful if you're confident that the called procedures work correctly.
- **Step Out (Ctrl+Shift+F8):** Executes the remaining lines in the current procedure and then pauses. This is useful when you want to finish the current procedure quickly and return to the calling procedure.

Inspecting variables with the Locals Window

The Locals window displays all variables in the current scope and their values. This is very useful for understanding the state of your macro at any point in time. To open the Locals window, go to *View > Locals Window* in the VBA editor.

Using the Immediate Window

The Immediate window lets you execute VBA statements on the fly and print variable values. To open the Immediate window, go to *View > Immediate Window* in the VBA editor. Here's how to use it:

```
' To print the value of a variable
Debug.Print myVariable


' To change the value of a variable
myVariable = 10
```

Error Handling with Line Numbers

For more advanced error handling, you can use line numbers in your code to determine exactly where an error occurred. This can be especially helpful for debugging large procedures.

```
Sub AdvancedErrorHandling()
    On Error GoTo ErrorHandler


    10 Debug.Print "Start of macro"
    20 Dim x As Integer
    30 x = 1 / 0 ' This will cause an error
```

```
40 MsgBox "This message won't be displayed due to the
error above."

Exit Sub

ErrorHandler:
    MsgBox "Error at line " & Erl & ": " & Err.Description
End Sub
```

In this example:

- The Erl function returns the line number where the error occurred.

Using Assert statements

Assert statements are useful for checking conditions that should always be true in your code. If an assertion fails, it indicates a bug in your program.

```
Sub UseAssertions()
    Debug.Assert 1 + 1 = 2 ' This will pass
    Debug.Assert 1 + 1 = 3 ' This will fail and pause
execution
End Sub
```

In this example:

- The *Debug.Assert* statement checks if the condition is true. If it's not, the debugger pauses execution.

Handling unexpected errors

Sometimes, errors might occur that you didn't anticipate. Using a generic error handler at the end of your procedures can help you catch and log these unexpected errors.

```
Sub GenericErrorHandler()
    On Error GoTo ErrorHandler

    ' Your code here

    Exit Sub

ErrorHandler:
```

```
    MsgBox "An unexpected error occurred: " &
Err.Description
    Resume Next
End Sub
```

In this example:

- The error handler catches any unexpected errors and displays a message box.

Putting it all together

Let's create a comprehensive example that demonstrates robust error handling and debugging techniques.

```
Sub ComprehensiveExample()
    On Error GoTo ErrorHandler

    Debug.Print "Starting macro..."

    ' Set a breakpoint on the following line
    Dim x As Integer
    x = 1 / 0 ' This will cause an error

    Debug.Print "This message won't be displayed due to
the error above."

    Exit Sub

ErrorHandler:
    Debug.Print "Error occurred at line " & Erl & ": " &
Err.Description
    LogError "Error at line " & Erl & ": " &
Err.Description
    Resume Next
End Sub

Sub LogError(errorMessage As String)
    Dim logFile As String
```

```
logFile = "C:\path\to\your\error_log.txt"

Dim fileNum As Integer
fileNum = FreeFile

Open logFile For Append As #fileNum
Print #fileNum, Now & " - " & errorMessage
Close #fileNum
End Sub
```

In this comprehensive example:

- We use the VBA debugger to step through the code and inspect variables.
- We handle errors with a structured error handler that logs errors to a file.
- We use the *Erl* function to determine the line number where an error occurred.

By mastering these error handling and debugging techniques, you can make your VBA macros more robust and easier to maintain. Keep practicing, and soon you'll be able to handle even the most complex debugging challenges with ease!

19. Optimizing VBA code

Writing efficient and fast VBA code is essential for creating robust macros that perform well, especially when dealing with large datasets or complex calculations. This chapter will cover techniques for improving macro performance and best practices for writing efficient VBA code.

Improving macro performance

Turn off screen updating

When running a macro, Excel updates the screen frequently, which can slow down performance. Turning off screen updating can speed up your macro:

```
Sub TurnOffScreenUpdating()
    Application.ScreenUpdating = False

    ' Your macro code here
```

```
        Application.ScreenUpdating = True
    End Sub
```

In this example:

- *Application.ScreenUpdating = False* turns off screen updating.
- Remember to turn it back on with *Application.ScreenUpdating = True* at the end of your macro.

Disable automatic calculations

Excel recalculates formulas whenever a change is made. Disabling automatic calculations during the macro can improve performance:

```
    Sub DisableAutomaticCalculations()
        Application.Calculation = xlCalculationManual

        ' Your macro code here

        Application.Calculation = xlCalculationAutomatic
        Application.Calculate ' Ensure all formulas are
    recalculated
    End Sub
```

In this example:

- *Application.Calculation = xlCalculationManual* turns off automatic calculations.
- *Application.Calculation = xlCalculationAutomatic* turns them back on at the end.

Use efficient data structures

Using arrays instead of directly manipulating ranges can significantly speed up your code:

```
    Sub UseArraysForEfficiency()
        Dim ws As Worksheet
        Set ws = ThisWorkbook.Sheets("Sheet1")

        Dim dataRange As Range
        Set dataRange = ws.Range("A1:A1000")
```

```
Dim dataArray() As Variant
dataArray = dataRange.Value ' Load range into array

Dim i As Long
For i = 1 To UBound(dataArray)
    dataArray(i, 1) = dataArray(i, 1) * 2 ' Example
operation
Next i

dataRange.Value = dataArray ' Write array back to
range
End Sub
```

In this example:

- We load a range into an array, perform operations on the array, and then write the array back to the range.

Avoid using *Select* and *Activate*

Using *Select* and *Activate* can slow down your code. Instead, work directly with objects:

```
Sub AvoidSelectAndActivate()
    Dim ws As Worksheet
    Set ws = ThisWorkbook.Sheets("Sheet1")

    ' Instead of ws.Select
    ws.Range("A1").Value = "Hello"

    ' Instead of ws.Range("A1").Select
    ws.Range("A1").Interior.Color = RGB(255, 255, 0)
End Sub
```

In this example:

- We work directly with the worksheet and range objects without selecting or activating them.

Best practices for writing efficient VBA code

Use descriptive variable names

Using descriptive variable names makes your code easier to understand and maintain:

```vba
Sub UseDescriptiveVariableNames()
    Dim salesTotal As Double
    salesTotal = 1000.0

    Dim salesTaxRate As Double
    salesTaxRate = 0.07

    Dim salesTax As Double
    salesTax = salesTotal * salesTaxRate
End Sub
```

In this example:

- Variable names like *salesTotal*, *salesTaxRate*, and *salesTax* make the code easier to read and understand.

Comment your code

Adding comments to your code helps explain what it does, making it easier to maintain:

```vba
Sub CommentYourCode()
    ' Calculate the total sales tax
    Dim salesTotal As Double
    salesTotal = 1000.0

    Dim salesTaxRate As Double
    salesTaxRate = 0.07

    ' Multiply total sales by the tax rate to get the
sales tax
    Dim salesTax As Double
    salesTax = salesTotal * salesTaxRate
End Sub
```

In this example:

- Comments explain the purpose of the code and the calculations being performed.

Use constants for fixed values

Using constants for fixed values makes your code easier to maintain and reduces the risk of errors:

```
Sub UseConstants()
    Const SALES_TAX_RATE As Double = 0.07

    Dim salesTotal As Double
    salesTotal = 1000.0

    Dim salesTax As Double
    salesTax = salesTotal * SALES_TAX_RATE
End Sub
```

In this example:

- The constant *SALES_TAX_RATE* is used for the sales tax rate, making it easy to update if needed.

Optimize loops

Minimize the number of iterations in loops by using the most efficient loop structure and avoiding unnecessary calculations inside the loop:

```
Sub OptimizeLoops()
    Dim ws As Worksheet
    Set ws = ThisWorkbook.Sheets("Sheet1")

    Dim lastRow As Long
    lastRow = ws.Cells(ws.Rows.Count, "A").End(xlUp).Row

    Dim i As Long
    For i = 1 To lastRow
        ws.Cells(i, 2).Value = ws.Cells(i, 1).Value * 2 '
Example operation
    Next i
End Sub
```

In this example:

- We minimize the number of iterations by finding the last row only once, outside the loop.

Avoid using variants unnecessarily

Using specific data types instead of *Variant* improves performance and helps catch errors:

```
Sub AvoidVariants()
    Dim salesTotal As Double
    salesTotal = 1000.0

    Dim salesTaxRate As Double
    salesTaxRate = 0.07

    Dim salesTax As Double
    salesTax = salesTotal * salesTaxRate
End Sub
```

In this example:

- We use specific data types like Double instead of Variant for better performance and type safety.

Putting it all together

Let's create a comprehensive example that demonstrates these optimization techniques and best practices.

```
Sub OptimizeMacro()
    ' Turn off screen updating and automatic calculations
    Application.ScreenUpdating = False
    Application.Calculation = xlCalculationManual

    Dim ws As Worksheet
    Set ws = ThisWorkbook.Sheets("Sheet1")

    ' Load data into an array for faster processing
    Dim dataRange As Range
    Set dataRange = ws.Range("A1:A1000")
    Dim dataArray() As Variant
    dataArray = dataRange.Value
```

```
' Process data in the array
Dim i As Long
For i = 1 To UBound(dataArray)
    dataArray(i, 1) = dataArray(i, 1) * 2 ' Example
operation
Next i

' Write the processed data back to the worksheet
dataRange.Value = dataArray

' Turn on screen updating and automatic calculations
Application.ScreenUpdating = True
Application.Calculation = xlCalculationAutomatic
Application.Calculate ' Ensure all formulas are
recalculated
End Sub
```

In this comprehensive example:

- We turn off screen updating and automatic calculations to improve performance.
- We load data into an array, process it, and then write it back to the worksheet.
- We follow best practices by using descriptive variable names, commenting the code, and avoiding unnecessary *Variant* types.

By mastering these techniques for optimizing VBA code, you can create faster, more efficient macros that are easier to maintain and debug. Keep practicing, and soon you'll be able to write optimized VBA code with ease!

20. User interface customization

Customizing the user interface (UI) in Excel can greatly enhance your productivity by providing quick access to your macros and creating intuitive user interactions. In this chapter, we'll explore how to create custom ribbons and toolbars, as well as how to develop user forms and dialog boxes.

Creating custom ribbons and toolbars

Custom ribbons

Custom ribbons allow you to add your own tabs and buttons to the Excel ribbon, making it easier to run your macros. Here's how to create a custom ribbon using VBA:

1. Open the Custom UI Editor:

- Download and install the *Office Custom UI Editor*.

2. Add custom XML:

- Open your Excel workbook in the *Custom UI Editor*.

- Add the following XML code to create a custom tab with a button:

```
<customUI
xmlns="http://schemas.microsoft.com/office/2009/07/customui">
  <ribbon>
    <tabs>
      <tab id="customTab" label="My Custom Tab">
        <group id="customGroup" label="My Custom Group">
          <button id="customButton" label="Run Macro"
onAction="RunMyMacro" />
        </group>
      </tab>
    </tabs>
  </ribbon>
</customUI>
```

3. Add VBA code:

- In Excel, open the VBA editor (Alt + F11) and add the following code to a module:

```
Sub RunMyMacro(control As IRibbonControl)
    MsgBox "Hello, this is your custom macro!"
End Sub
```

4. Save and reload:

- Save your workbook and reopen it in Excel. You should see your custom tab and button.

In this example:

- We create a custom ribbon tab with a button that runs a macro when clicked.

Custom toolbars

If you prefer the classic toolbar approach, you can create custom toolbars using VBA. Here's how:

```
Sub CreateCustomToolbar()
    Dim cmdBar As CommandBar
    Dim cmdButton As CommandBarButton

    ' Delete existing custom toolbar if it exists
    On Error Resume Next
    Application.CommandBars("MyToolbar").Delete
    On Error GoTo 0

    ' Create a new custom toolbar
    Set cmdBar =
Application.CommandBars.Add(Name:="MyToolbar",
Position:=msoBarTop, Temporary:=True)

    ' Add a button to the toolbar
    Set cmdButton =
cmdBar.Controls.Add(Type:=msoControlButton)
    With cmdButton
        .Caption = "Run Macro"
        .OnAction = "RunMyMacro"
        .Style = msoButtonCaption
    End With

    ' Show the toolbar
    cmdBar.Visible = True
End Sub

Sub RunMyMacro()
    MsgBox "Hello, this is your custom macro!"
End Sub
```

In this example:

- We create a custom toolbar with a button that runs a macro when clicked.

Developing user forms and dialog boxes

User forms and dialog boxes provide a more interactive way for users to input data and control your macros. Here's how to create and use them.

Creating a user form

1. **Add a user form:**

   o In the VBA editor, go to *Insert > UserForm* to add a new user form.

2. **Design the form:**

   o Use the toolbox to add controls (like text boxes, labels, and buttons) to the form.

   o Set the properties of each control (e.g., name, caption) using the properties window.

3. **Add code to the form:**

   o Double-click a control (e.g., a button) to open the code window and add your VBA code.

Here's an example of a simple user form with a text box and a button:

1. **Design the Form:**

   o Add a text box (*txtName*) and a button (*btnSubmit*).

2. **Add Code:**

   ```
   ' UserForm Code
   Private Sub btnSubmit_Click()
       MsgBox "Hello, " & txtName.Value & "!"
   End Sub
   ```

3. **Show the form:**
   o Create a macro to show the form:

   ```
   Sub ShowUserForm()
   ```

```
        UserForm1.Show
    End Sub
```

In this example:

- The user enters their name in the text box, and clicking the button displays a greeting message.

Developing dialog boxes

Dialog boxes can be used to prompt the user for simple inputs. Here's how to create an input box and a message box:

Input Box

```
    Sub ShowInputBox()
        Dim userName As String
        userName = InputBox("Please enter your name:")

        If userName <> "" Then
            MsgBox "Hello, " & userName & "!"
        Else
            MsgBox "You didn't enter your name."
        End If
    End Sub
```

In this example:

- An input box prompts the user to enter their name, and a message box displays a greeting.

Message Box

```
    Sub ShowMessageBox()
        Dim response As VbMsgBoxResult
        response = MsgBox("Do you want to continue?", vbYesNo
+ vbQuestion, "Continue?")

        If response = vbYes Then
            MsgBox "You chose to continue."
        Else
            MsgBox "You chose not to continue."
        End If
```

```
      End Sub
```

In this example:

- A message box asks the user if they want to continue and displays a response based on their choice.

Putting it all together

Let's create a comprehensive example that combines custom ribbons, user forms, and dialog boxes.

1. Create a custom ribbon button:

- Use the *Custom UI Editor* to add a button to your ribbon that shows a user form.

```
<customUI
xmlns="http://schemas.microsoft.com/office/2009/07/customui">
    <ribbon>
      <tabs>
        <tab id="customTab" label="My Custom Tab">
          <group id="customGroup" label="My Custom Group">
            <button id="customButton" label="Show Form"
onAction="ShowUserForm" />
          </group>
        </tab>
      </tabs>
    </ribbon>
</customUI>
```

2. Create the user form:

- Add a user form with a text box (*txtName*), a button (*btnSubmit*), and a label (*lblMessage*).

3. Add code to the form:

```
      ' UserForm Code
      Private Sub btnSubmit_Click()
          If txtName.Value <> "" Then
              lblMessage.Caption = "Hello, " & txtName.Value &
"!"
          Else
```

```
            lblMessage.Caption = "Please enter your name."
        End If
    End Sub
```

4. Show the form:

```
    Sub ShowUserForm(control As IRibbonControl)
        UserForm1.Show
    End Sub
```

In this comprehensive example:

- We create a custom ribbon with a button that shows a user form.
- The user form prompts the user to enter their name and displays a personalized greeting message.

By mastering these techniques for customizing the user interface in Excel, you can create more intuitive and user-friendly macros. Keep practicing, and soon you'll be able to design and implement complex UI customizations with ease!

Chapter 8: Case studies and real-world examples

21. Case study: automating financial reports in Excel

Automating financial reports can save you a significant amount of time and ensure that your data is always accurate and up-to-date. In this chapter, we'll walk through a real-world example of how to automate a financial report in Excel using VBA. This case study will cover the entire process, from setting up your data to generating the final report.

Real-world example of a financial report automation

Scenario

Imagine you work for a company that needs to generate a monthly financial report. This report includes data on revenues, expenses, and net profit. The data is stored in multiple sheets within an Excel workbook, and you need to compile it into a summary report.

Step 1: Setting Up Your Data

First, let's set up our data in Excel. We'll have three sheets: *Revenues*, *Expenses*, and *Summary*.

- **Revenues**: Contains data on monthly revenues.
    - o   Columns: *Date, Revenue*
- **Expenses**: Contains data on monthly expenses.
    - o   Columns: *Date, Expense*
- **Summary**: This will be our summary report.
    - o   Columns: *Date, Total Revenue, Total Expense, Net Profit*

Step 2: Writing the VBA Code

We'll write VBA code to automate the process of generating the summary report. The code will:

1.   Read data from the *Revenues* and *Expenses* sheets.

2. Calculate the total revenue, total expense, and net profit for each month.

3. Write the calculated data to the *Summary* sheet.

Here's the VBA code to accomplish this:

```
Sub GenerateFinancialReport()
    ' Declare variables
    Dim wsRevenues As Worksheet
    Dim wsExpenses As Worksheet
    Dim wsSummary As Worksheet
    Dim lastRowRevenues As Long
    Dim lastRowExpenses As Long
    Dim lastRowSummary As Long
    Dim i As Long, j As Long

    ' Set worksheets
    Set wsRevenues = ThisWorkbook.Sheets("Revenues")
    Set wsExpenses = ThisWorkbook.Sheets("Expenses")
    Set wsSummary = ThisWorkbook.Sheets("Summary")

    ' Find the last rows of data
    lastRowRevenues =
wsRevenues.Cells(wsRevenues.Rows.Count, "A").End(xlUp).Row
    lastRowExpenses =
wsExpenses.Cells(wsExpenses.Rows.Count, "A").End(xlUp).Row

    ' Clear previous summary data
    wsSummary.Range("A2:D" &
wsSummary.Rows.Count).ClearContents

    ' Copy headers to the summary sheet
    wsSummary.Range("A1:D1").Value = Array("Date", "Total
Revenue", "Total Expense", "Net Profit")

    ' Loop through the revenues data and copy to the
summary sheet
```

```vba
    For i = 2 To lastRowRevenues
        wsSummary.Cells(i, 1).Value = wsRevenues.Cells(i,
1).Value ' Date
        wsSummary.Cells(i, 2).Value = wsRevenues.Cells(i,
2).Value ' Revenue
    Next i


    ' Loop through the expenses data and copy to the
summary sheet
    For j = 2 To lastRowExpenses
        ' Find matching date in summary sheet
        For i = 2 To lastRowRevenues
            If wsExpenses.Cells(j, 1).Value =
wsSummary.Cells(i, 1).Value Then
                wsSummary.Cells(i, 3).Value =
wsExpenses.Cells(j, 2).Value ' Expense
                Exit For
            End If
        Next i
    Next j


    ' Calculate Net Profit
    lastRowSummary = wsSummary.Cells(wsSummary.Rows.Count,
"A").End(xlUp).Row
    For i = 2 To lastRowSummary
        wsSummary.Cells(i, 4).Value = wsSummary.Cells(i,
2).Value - wsSummary.Cells(i, 3).Value
    Next i


    ' Autofit columns
    wsSummary.Columns("A:D").AutoFit


    MsgBox "Financial report generated successfully!",
    vbInformation
    End Sub
```

In this example:

- We set references to the *Revenues, Expenses*, and *Summary* sheets.

- We find the last rows of data in the *Revenues* and *Expenses* sheets.

- We clear any previous summary data and set up headers in the *Summary* sheet.

- We loop through the *Revenues* data and copy it to the *Summary* sheet.

- We loop through the *Expenses* data and find matching dates in the *Summary* sheet, copying the expenses data accordingly.

- We calculate the net profit for each month and write it to the *Summary* sheet.

- Finally, we autofit the columns and display a message box indicating that the report has been generated successfully.

Step 3: Running the Macro

To run the macro:

1. Press *Alt + F8* to open the macro dialog box.

2. Select *GenerateFinancialReport* and click *Run*.

Summary

By automating the financial report, you save time and ensure that your data is accurate and consistently formatted. This process can be adapted to various types of reports, making it a versatile tool in your Excel toolkit.

This case study demonstrates how VBA can streamline complex tasks, allowing you to focus on analysis rather than data compilation. Keep practicing these techniques, and you'll be able to automate a wide range of reporting tasks with ease!

22. Case study: dynamic document generation in Word

Creating dynamic documents in Word based on user input can save you time and ensure consistency. In this chapter, we'll walk through a real-world example of how to automate the creation of dynamic documents in Word using VBA. We'll cover the entire process, from capturing user input to generating the final document.

Automating the creation of dynamic documents based on user input

Scenario

Imagine you work for a company that needs to generate personalized letters for clients. Each letter includes the client's name, address, and a personalized message. Instead of manually creating each letter, you can automate the process using VBA.

Step 1: Setting up the user form

First, let's create a user form to capture user input.

1. **Add a user form:**

   o In the VBA editor, go to *Insert > UserForm* to add a new user form.

2. **Design the form:**

   o Add text boxes for the client's name (*txtName*), address (*txtAddress*), and message (*txtMessage*).

   o Add a button (*btnGenerate*) to generate the document.

3. **Add code to the form:**

```
Private Sub btnGenerate_Click()
    Call GenerateDocument(txtName.Value, txtAddress.Value,
txtMessage.Value)
End Sub
```

In this example:

- The button click event calls the *GenerateDocument* subroutine, passing the user input as parameters.

Step 2: Writing the VBA code

We'll write VBA code to generate the Word document based on the user input.

1. **Create the *GenerateDocument* Subroutine:**

```vba
Sub GenerateDocument(clientName As String, clientAddress As
String, clientMessage As String)
    Dim wordApp As Object
    Dim wordDoc As Object
    Dim filePath As String

    ' Create a new instance of Word
    Set wordApp = CreateObject("Word.Application")
    wordApp.Visible = True

    ' Add a new document
    Set wordDoc = wordApp.Documents.Add

    ' Add content to the document
    With wordDoc
        .Content.Text = "Dear " & clientName & "," & vbCrLf &
vbCrLf & _
                        clientMessage & vbCrLf & vbCrLf & _
                        "Sincerely," & vbCrLf & _
                        "Your Company Name" & vbCrLf & _
                        clientAddress
    End With

    ' Save the document
    filePath = "C:\path\to\save\Document_" & clientName &
".docx"
    wordDoc.SaveAs2 filePath

    ' Clean up
    wordDoc.Close
    wordApp.Quit
    Set wordDoc = Nothing
    Set wordApp = Nothing

    MsgBox "Document generated successfully!", vbInformation
End Sub
```

In this example:

- We create a new instance of Word and add a new document.
- We add content to the document using the user input.
- We save the document with a filename that includes the client's name.
- We display a message box indicating that the document was generated successfully.

Step 3: Running the user form

To run the user form:

1. Create a macro to show the user form:

```
Sub ShowUserForm()
    UserForm1.Show
End Sub
```

2. Press *Alt + F8* to open the macro dialog box.
3. Select *ShowUserForm* and click *Run*.

Summary

By automating the creation of dynamic documents, you save time and ensure that each document is personalized and formatted consistently. This process can be adapted to various types of documents, making it a versatile tool in your Word toolkit.

This case study demonstrates how VBA can streamline complex tasks, allowing you to focus on more critical activities rather than repetitive document creation. Keep practicing these techniques, and you'll be able to automate a wide range of document generation tasks with ease!

23. Case study: automated presentation updates

Keeping PowerPoint presentations up-to-date with the latest data can be a tedious task, especially if you have to do it regularly. Automating this process with VBA can save you a lot of time and ensure that your presentations always reflect the most current information. In this chapter, we'll walk through a real-world example of how to automate PowerPoint presentation updates using data from Excel.

Keeping PowerPoint presentations up-to-date with the latest data

Scenario

Imagine you work for a company that needs to update a monthly sales presentation with the latest sales figures from an Excel spreadsheet. Instead of manually updating the slides each month, you can automate the process to ensure accuracy and save time.

Step 1: Setting up your data

First, let's set up our data in Excel. We'll have a sheet named *SalesData* containing the latest sales figures.

- **SalesData**: Contains monthly sales data.

  o   Columns: *Month, Sales*

Step 2: Writing the VBA Code

We'll write VBA code to automate the process of updating the PowerPoint presentation with the latest sales data from Excel.

1.   **Prepare the PowerPoint Presentation**

    Ensure your PowerPoint presentation has placeholders or specific locations where the sales data will be updated. For example, you might have a slide with a table or text boxes that display the sales figures.

2.   **Create the VBA Macro in Excel**

    Here's the VBA code to update the PowerPoint presentation with data from the Excel sheet:

```
Sub UpdatePowerPointWithData()
    Dim excelApp As Object
    Dim excelWorkbook As Object
    Dim salesRange As Range
    Dim pptApp As Object
    Dim pptPresentation As Object
    Dim pptSlide As Object
    Dim pptShape As Object
```

```vba
    Dim i As Integer

    ' Path to the files
    Dim excelFilePath As String
    Dim pptFilePath As String
    excelFilePath = "C:\path\to\your\SalesData.xlsx"
    pptFilePath = "C:\path\to\your\SalesPresentation.pptx"

    ' Create a new instance of Excel and open the workbook
    Set excelApp = CreateObject("Excel.Application")
    Set excelWorkbook = excelApp.Workbooks.Open(excelFilePath)

    ' Define the range of sales data to copy
    Set salesRange =
excelWorkbook.Sheets("SalesData").Range("A2:B13") ' Adjust the
range as needed

    ' Create a new instance of PowerPoint and open the
presentation
    Set pptApp = CreateObject("PowerPoint.Application")
    pptApp.Visible = True
    Set pptPresentation =
pptApp.Presentations.Open(pptFilePath)

    ' Loop through each row of the sales data and update the
presentation
    For i = 1 To salesRange.Rows.Count
        ' Assume each row corresponds to a specific slide and
update accordingly
        Set pptSlide = pptPresentation.Slides(i)

        ' Update slide content (e.g., text boxes or table
cells)
        ' This example assumes the data goes into a text box
named "SalesTextBox"
        For Each pptShape In pptSlide.Shapes
```

```
            If pptShape.Name = "SalesTextBox" Then
                 pptShape.TextFrame.TextRange.Text = "Month: "
& salesRange.Cells(i, 1).Value & _

                                          vbCrLf &
"Sales: $" & Format(salesRange.Cells(i, 2).Value, "#,##0")
            End If
        Next pptShape
    Next i


    ' Save and close the PowerPoint presentation
    pptPresentation.Save
    pptPresentation.Close

    ' Clean up
    excelWorkbook.Close SaveChanges:=False
    excelApp.Quit
    Set salesRange = Nothing
    Set excelWorkbook = Nothing
    Set excelApp = Nothing
    Set pptSlide = Nothing
    Set pptPresentation = Nothing
    Set pptApp = Nothing


    MsgBox "PowerPoint presentation updated successfully!",
    vbInformation
End Sub
```

In this example:

- We open the Excel workbook containing the sales data.
- We define the range of sales data to be copied.
- We open the PowerPoint presentation.
- We loop through each row of the sales data, updating corresponding slides in the PowerPoint presentation. In this example, we assume each row corresponds to a specific slide and each slide contains a text box named *SalesTextBox* where the sales data will be inserted.
- We save and close the PowerPoint presentation.

Step 3: Running the macro

To run the macro:

1. Press *Alt + F8* to open the macro dialog box.

2. Select *UpdatePowerPointWithData* and click *Run*.

Summary

By automating the process of updating your PowerPoint presentation with the latest data from Excel, you ensure that your presentation is always up-to-date without the need for manual updates. This not only saves time but also reduces the risk of errors.

This case study demonstrates how VBA can streamline the task of keeping your presentations current, allowing you to focus on delivering impactful and accurate presentations. Keep practicing these techniques, and you'll be able to automate a wide range of presentation tasks with ease!

www.ingramcontent.com/pod-product-compliance
Lightning Source LLC
LaVergne TN
LVHW051343050326
832903LV00031B/3713